HOW TO WIN YOUR VOTE

HOW TO WIN YOUR
VOTE

A TRUE STORY OF **POLITICAL MARKETING** IN ACTION

BY

KURT GASSNER

My-mindguide.com

How to win your Vote
Kurt Gassner

Impressum
My-mindguide – The publishing trademarke of trendguide Capital GmbH, Klenzestr. 42a, 80469 Munich, Germany.

Reg. Nr. HRB Munich 206639, VAT 152 123 159, CEO: Kurt Friedrich Gassner
Web: www.my-mindguide.com, mail: gassner@my-mindguide.com

Paperback ISBN: 978-3-98793-918-1
Hardback ISBN: 978-3-949978-95-1

Table of Contents

Election Campaign

My-mindguide.com

Campaign strategies for upcoming elections

My-mindguide.com

PREFACE

Despite several incidents over the years, the study of politics remains in an unsatisfactory state. Representative democracy is often regarded as the finest form of administration in Europe and America, yet individuals who have first-hand experience with it are frequently disillusioned and even concerned.

Democracy is a big word meant to indicate the reign of the people. Democracy rests upon the principles of majority rule and individual rights. However, because it is a system of government by the whole population, it becomes considerably more complicated. People's thoughts, especially the ideas twinkling in young people's minds, are filled with age-old questions. Who really guides the people? Who suggests the ideas and images in connection with the government? Examining these things cuts down even deeper as it reveals the astonishing power of marketing. Yes, marketing and dark psychology often go pari passu.

With this book, I hope to emphasise that we are inarguably affected by marketing in today's commercial and media-driven world. We are often unable to make decisions in our own best interests. We've been brainwashed.

When Jim Morrison declared, **"Whoever controls the media controls the mind, and so controls the people,"** he was absolutely correct. Who do you believe has power over the media in the real world? Take a glance behind the curtain of the major media conglomerates; who is in charge of them?

Media and its enormous role in contemporary society cannot be underestimated. The evolution and progress of media and mass media, as well as media-related professions, are inextricably linked to its role. We can see avid mobilisation in today's contemporary society, which shapes the fabric of decision-making capacity when we look at mechanisation and operationalisation in society as a whole. It also presents in the arena of politics and how different forms of media create opportunities and encourage both political campaigns and activism. The media is actively involved in gathering political influence. For example, by altering election results through direct and indirect brand awareness mechanisms, and utilizing the political media complex, emphasising the notion that "whoever controls the media controls the mind."

But, what I am painting shouldn't in the slightest sense suggest that I favour totalitarian systems. I certainly don't force the idea of an authoritarian regime. However, we must be aware in our western world—especially with the concepts of the metaverse, social media, and influencers—that we awoke one day to find that only the label is different.

We're puppets on a string, whether we realize it or not. Investigate who the big campaigns' spin doctors, campaign strategists, ad agencies, and public relations firms are. What methods do they employ to persuade people to vote in their favour? In this book, I provide general answers to questions like these. While anyone who can read English squiggles can read this book, I wrote it primarily as a source of insight and experience for rising adults and the elderly, people with political interests, influencers, and marketing people involved in politics and business. I sincerely hope you enjoy reading it and that it piques your interest and makes you think.

Election Campaign

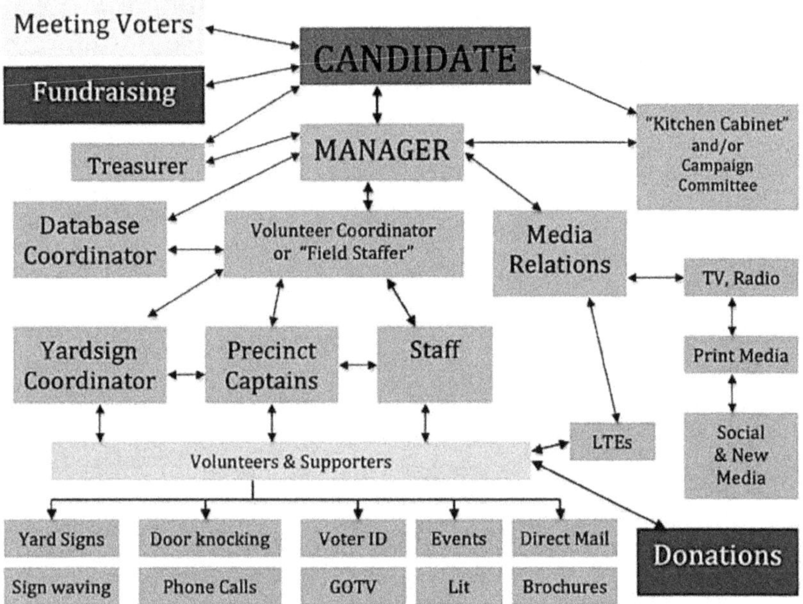

Chapter 1

My Little Story

Before I get to the actual content of this book, I have to delve quite a bit into the past. I would dare to say that this personal experience, among other reasons, was instrumental in my decision to write this book.

About nineteen years ago, my accountant visited me in my office and asked the following question ‚Do you think I should run for mayor? They asked me about it.'

That simple question lead to an intense friendship and collaboration - and it subsequently gave us 4 successful election campaigns:

First, let me give you a brief overview of the scenario.

Kitzbühel, in the west of Austria, is seen by many as the Monaco of the Alps. The city is a well-known winter sports resort, famous for the so called Hahnenkamm race, which takes place every year. The streets of the historic centre are lined with exquisite shops and cafés. The Kitzbühel Museum houses paintings by local artist Alfons Walde and commemorates the history of the city, as well as winter sports in the entire region.

So, the city of Kitzbühel attracts wealthy people and celebrities from all over the world and is known for hosting the most spectacular ski racing event in the world.

I would argue that these aspects make the position of Kitzbühel's mayor a very coveted one.

Unfortunately the high density of millionaires sometimes leads to conflicts with the local population when it comes to housing and high living costs.

Well, let's have a look at the balance sheet of our elections:

Election #1, 2004: My friend, although largely unknown to the public, succeeded in replacing the incumbent mayor and winning a majority in the municipal council within only 4 months.

At that time I was running a PR agency in Kitzbühel and Munich and I firmly believed that I had the skills, the know-how and the possibilities to turn the unimaginable into a reasonable possibility.

How did we achive this? I will explain it to you in the next chapters.

Election #2, 2010: This election victory turned out to be totally overwhelming: 80% of the people voted for the mayor and the majority in the municipal council expanded as well. Of course, the candidate and his entire team were excellent, but nevertheless the result was also based on efficient political marketing.

Election #3, 2016: We got the absolute majority once more, both in the municipal council and for the mayor's office!

What was even more amazing: We were the only city in Tirol to achieve this outstanding result.

Election #4, February 2022: We won again ... for the fourth time in a row!

Our mayor was re-elected, with more than 50% of the people's votes. His parliamentary group won nine out of nineteen mandates.

This time we even took the victory against all odds.

The conservative party in Austria had been shattered by scandals this year. Our country was lead by three different chancellors within four weeks! Furthermore, we had to deal with the Covid 19 pandemic and a huge coalition of mass media (TV) that ganged up against us - and yet we achieved a result that everyone was proud of.

Thank you! For me, this mission is accomplished! If I ever wanted to prove something as a creative mind in the marketing and communications industry, I have done it right here.

I wish the indefatigable mayor the best of luck for the upcoming six years!

In the next few chapters I will explain the facts, principles, secrets, processes and tactics that have helped us and can certainly help anybody who conscientiously applies them in relation to their goals. These proven concepts will be immensely helpful to anyone who wants to venture into politics.

****

Bei der Gemeinderatswahl am 27. Februar wollen die Liste UK und die FPÖ in Kitzbühel koppeln.

Gemeinsam gegen Winkler

In Kitzbühel wollen die Liste UK und die FPÖ koppeln. Auch SPÖ und Grüne wurden eingeladen, erteilten aber eine Absage.

Von Harald Angerer

Kitzbühel – Es ist ein Ziel, welches in Kitzbühel die SPÖ, Grüne, FPÖ und die Liste Unabhängige Kitzbüheler (UK) eint. Sie alle wollen die absolute Mehrheit von Bürgermeister Klaus Winkler und seiner ÖVP brechen. Die UK hatte deshalb alle drei anderen Listen dazu eingeladen, mit ihnen zu koppeln. Durch die Verknüpfung (Koppelung) von zwei oder mehreren Listen werden deren Reststimmen gebündelt. Dieses Potenzial kann bei der Auszählung zusätzliche Mandate bringen. „In den

Gemeinderats-Wahl 2022

Vorgesprächen mit SPÖ, FPÖ und den Grünen haben alle die verloren gegangene Diskussionsbereitschaft der ÖVP durch ihre absolute Mehrheit im Gemeinderat seit zwölf Jahren beklagt", begründet UK-Spitzenkandidat Andreas Fuchs-Marschitz die Bestrebungen zu koppeln.

sich nur eine Koppelung mit den Grünen vorstellen, hier würden die Gespräche laufen. Auch die Grünen gaben der UK einen Korb. „Wenn wirklich die gesamte Opposition mitgemacht hätte, wäre es ein Thema gewesen, aber so nicht", sagt GR Rudi Wichmoser von den Grünen.

Zugesagt hat hingegen die FPÖ. „Wir nehmen das Angebot der UK an und werden mit ihnen koppeln", sagt FPÖ-Stadtparteiobmann LA Alexander Gamper. Noch im Jahr 2016 kritisierte die FPÖ die SPÖ und Grüne, weil diese bei der letzten Wahl gekoppelt hatten. Damals wetterte die FPÖ „Koppeln ist Wählertäuschung." Das sieht man nun anders. Für die Wahl 2022 gilt „Der Zweck heiligt die Mittel", wie Gamper sagt. Es gehe, die Vormachtstellung der ÖVP zu brechen.

Zwischen der FPÖ und dem UK-Spitzenkandidaten Fuchs-Marschitz gibt es auch eine alte Verbindung. So war er bereits Mitglied der FPÖ-Seniorpartei. „Ich war immer schon ein politischer Mensch und damals war es

A Political Campaign

"The most precious resource in any campaign is the candidate's time.

My-mindguide.com

2004

My-mindguide.com

2004

Vorsprung für Kitzbühel
elect 2004_folder
elect.2004_digital
elect.2004_direct mail
Packen wir's an
election 2004
Danke
Jetzt gilt's
Winkler
elect.2004_runoff
Der Selbst-Bedienungstrick!
election 2004_ attac campaign
"Wenn es ungesetzlich ist, dann ändern wir die Gesetze"
election 2004_ attac camp

election 2004

election 2004

Die Gams
ist wieder
schwarz
Bericht
auf Seite
2 und 3

Der große Sieger Klaus Winkler

winner headlinine 2004

election 2010

Weiter
gemeinsam
voran!
Liste 1
Kitzbühel zuerst
Bürgermeisterliste Dr. Klaus
Winkler
elect.2010

Campaign 2022

election 2022 final

elect.2022 street poster

elect. 2022 street

elect.2022. last call

elect.2022 street camp

elect. 2022 -folder

elect.2022.team

My-mindguide.com

Chapter Two

The People's Nature

I promised to shed additional light on the elements and secrets that made all of the events of the last chapter on my friend, the Mayor, possible. Specifically, we'll look at human nature in this chapter. There is a deep philosophy about politics and how those who understand how to use them can change or influence the decisions of others. Humans are wired to listen to what they want to hear rather than the truth and do what they genuinely wish to rather than what should be done or is required. When a keen and deep-thinking politician grasps this principle, it becomes a powerful tool in their hands for swaying the public. Don't forget; we're talking about politics here.

Arguments about human nature have long been a hot topic in philosophy, and the concept continues to stir up controversy. Human nature refers to the natural inclinations and qualities that humans portray, including thinking, feeling, and behavior. I recently realised that humans can and will tolerate and suffer just as much as they can scream out for aid or change. Simply tell them what they want to hear and let them accomplish what they've always wanted to do. Humans are more impulsive than deliberate by nature. Nazi leader Hermann Göring explained how people can be made fearful and led to support a war they otherwise would oppose by stating:

> *"The people don't want war, but they can always be brought to the bidding of the leaders. This is easy. All you have to do is tell them they are being attacked and denounce the pacifists for lack of patriotism and for exposing the country to danger. It works the same in every country."*

Actors are more common than intellectuals among Homo sapiens. In the hands of pros, this is a powerful instrument. Whoever wants to base his political thinking on a re-examination of human nature's workings must first overcome his predisposition to overstate humanity's intellectuality.

We are prone to believe that every human action is the product of an intellectual process in which a man first considers the desired aim, then calculates the methods to achieve that end. Unfortunately, that is not as often the case as we would prefer.

Types of Natural Instincts

Throughout the years, humanity has shown a remarkable ability to adapt to various changes in its environment. Humans have survived because of their ability to respond physically and psychologically to a changing world while other species perished. The same survival strategies that helped our ancestors stay alive can also help us stay alive! However, if we don't comprehend and anticipate their presence, these survival mechanisms can also act against us. In a survival crisis, it's not strange that the average person will have some psychological reactions.

In politics, there are instincts and impulses (both from the masses and your opponents) that we must master to use when the opportunity arises. You'll have to train yourself to avoid displaying harmful inclinations that can leave you exposed to your opponents. This is more like a chess game, in which you alternate between white and black pieces. We know that the colour of your pieces has no bearing on whether or not you will win. It's all about principles and who can play the rules of the game the best.

We'll look at some of the primary internal reactions you and anyone around you (perhaps, your opponent) might have in response to the survival stressors mentioned earlier. Politics is a survival game, and surprisingly, the wisest, not the fittest, emerge victoriously.

Fear

Fear is our emotional reaction to potentially harmful situations that we feel could result in death, damage, or illness. This harm isn't restricted to physical injury, however. Threats to one's emotional and mental well-being can also cause worry. Fear can benefit a person attempting to survive if it pushes him to be cautious in situations where irresponsibility could result in injury. Unfortunately, terror can render a person immobile. It can make him so terrified that he fails to take the actions necessary for survival. When placed in strange circumstances under adverse conditions, most of us will experience some level of terror. This isn't something to be ashamed of! Each person must develop the ability to resist being overcome by fear. Ideally, through realistic training, we can acquire the knowledge and skills needed to increase our confidence and manage our fears.

Understanding Fear Tactics

Everyday life is a gamble that continuously changes with the passing of time. Life's uncertainties are lurking around every corner, waiting to pounce on us whether we're ready or not. Life is full of danger and terror, which can knock us off our feet with tragedy, surprise, and guilt. But, more crucially, danger and dread enable the human entity to harden itself to unthinkable situations that we never foresaw. We might begin to dig into the caverns of our own identities by comprehending fear.

Fear, an extremely distressing force of the human mind, can sway, distort, and rupture the human psyche's traditions. As we piece together a disturbing puzzle of digressing feeling, the mind, body, and soul succumb to its macabre crimes. On the other hand, this same dread can bring disparate people together to form an impenetrable fortress while also allowing us to comprehend our own personalities.

Fear has the power to alter people's attitudes but understanding how our anxieties are utilised in a planned and intentional way might mitigate its impacts.

Fear, for example, can sway voters toward a specific candidate or political party, a strategy that taps into our natural desire to seek safety in numbers. Furthermore, Albarracin and her colleagues discovered that fear-based messages are roughly twice as effective as fear-free messages in a meta-analysis (Psychological Bulletin, Vol. 141, No. 6, 2015).

"Getting people to think about things as part of a group is a big part of politics," says Christopher Federico, Ph.D., a political science and psychology professor at the University of Minnesota. Politicians that use this method must first demonstrate that they (or their party) are the ideal people to deal with a particular issue. Once that's established, scaring others about the problem can lead them to seek solace by joining the ranks of the most capable group.

Campaigns also employ fear to dissuade voters from voting for political opponents. This technique could include making false or deceptive remarks about the other candidate's qualifications or claiming that a victory for the opposition would spell doom. On a more intimate level, when a politician throws doubt on a challenger's physical or mental well-being, the purpose is frequently to instil dread in followers, causing them to doubt their competence.

In addition to driving votes, fear is also used to diminish voter turnout. "If someone is extremely worried about an election or a candidate, they may avoid consuming any information about the candidate or the election," explains Leonie Huddy, Ph.D., a political science professor at Stony Brook State University. "Because thinking about the election is overly aversive, this may extend to voting abstention." To reduce voter turnout among an opponent's supporters, raising worry about an election or candidate is a common approach (The Journal of Politics, Vol. 73, No. 1, 2011; Political Research Quarterly, Vol. 66, No. 2, 2013).

Keeping Fear in Check

Understanding the emotion of fear may be the greatest approach to avoid being manipulated. "Fear causes people to withdraw, take a step back, and be cautious," Federico explains. "Fear and worry cause us to pause and reconsider our actions. However, when we re-evaluate out of fear, we typically seek information that validates our belief that a threat exists—which isn't always the most true or objective information."

The idea is that you keep an eye on your fear while also using it to your advantage against the enemy. This was emphasised throughout our first-term playbook. The opponent must be terrified of you—all parts of you—from your appearance to your graceful demeanour to your forceful remarks. Sow fear in his heart such that he panics when he hears your name. When your opponent has an advantage over you, play it the other way around. The emotional terror that comes with fear turns off the prefrontal cortex or the part of our brain that thinks rationally. To put it another way, when we are overcome by fear, we cease to think. A population that stops thinking for itself is easily led, misled, and used.

What I'm depicting is not establishing a fear culture or fear-mongering; they're both wicked techniques. I'm merely sharing some useful guidelines and tactics with you.

Fear is both a facilitator and a teacher. While I refer to fear as a teacher, please note that it comes with a debilitating sense of loneliness and helplessness. A terrified person, on the other hand, is a learned person. Fear has taught you what you find comfortable or unpleasant since our continued survival is a result of being terrified.

The concept of inciting fear in the general public to achieve political or professional goals was created as a sociological paradigm by Frank Furedi and popularised more recently by American sociologist Barry Glassner. Fear has had a significant effect on people due to their intake of mass media. It continues to be the primary route of establishing fear in our modern political environment.

What do you think will happen, on the other hand, if you just expose people's eyes to verifiable facts about what their leader has been doing with them to free them from an incumbent's grip? When someone becomes aware of a situation or state of things, they take appropriate action. If facts are brought to light that stir a sense of fear in the public as relates to the incumbent, all you have to do is sit back and wait for them to change sides.

An excellent example of this would be Ukranian President Volodymyr Zelenskyy. As most people know, his country is embroiled in a bloody war initiated by Russia. Through speeches to world leaders, and even to the public via a message broadcast at the Grammys, Zelenskyy has inspired and galvanized entire nations and people to support him in a war of attrition against the Russians. Zelenskyy highlights the parallel between Putin-led Russia and Hitler-Era Germany. In doing so, he stirs up realistic fears among the populations of other Western nations – fear of Europe being plunged into a hot war with Russia, fear of a vicious dictator intent on dominating the continent, and fear that neighboring NATO nations may be the next to fall to Putin's iron rule. Highlighting this in one speech, Zelenskyy said,

> *"Everyone thinks that we are far away from America or Canada. No, we are in this zone of freedom. And when the limits of rights and freedoms are being violated and stepped on, then you have to protect us. Because we will come first. You will come second. Because the more this beast will eat, he wants more, more, and more."*

Statements such as this have been highly effective in reminding people worldwide what they stand to lose. So much so that those who might otherwise have remained on the side lines have been stirred to action by fear of what Russia might do next. In the West, many who listen to Zelenskyy's speeches and media related to the war in Ukraine have cut ties with Russia entirely, including Russian culture. Bottles of Russian vodka are dumped down sinks in American restaurants. Russian music and literature is spurned. Global companies have pulled out of the Russian marketplace. This is a side effect of fear – it can be contagious. Russia's war of aggression was not committed by the Russian people, but by their leader, yet their entire nation suffers the consequence of global ostracization.

Beyond instilling realistic fear in those you seek support from, candidates must also come to terms with fear they themselves experience. When preparing for an election, the position of mayor in our case, embracing your fears gives you the feeling of being in control of your emotions. There's nothing like knowing who you are and understanding what makes you tick, jump, swear, grin, laugh, and cry. It is critical to own and understand your body and mind to succeed. Being terrified does not lead to success, but learning through fear is one way to attain information. As we all prepare for the risks of the world, knowing oneself can bring useful insights into the nuts and bolts of your psychology and maybe allow you to understand your opponents better, as well.

Anxiety

Anxiety is a feeling linked to fear. Because it is natural for us to be fearful (as it was for my friend when he first ran for mayor), it is also natural for us to feel anxious. When confronted with potentially harmful circumstances, anxiety can be an unpleasant, nervous feeling (physical, mental, and emotional). However, when anxiety is employed in a healthy way, it motivates us to take action to eliminate, or at the very least manage, the threats that are a danger to our survival. There would be little motivation to make changes in our lives if we were never anxious.

In a survival race (such as running for a political position), a person minimises his anxiety by completing actions to ensure that he survives the ordeal. As he lessens his anxiety, he also gain control over the source of his uneasiness: his fears. Anxiety is beneficial in this form; nevertheless, it can also be harmful. Anxiety can overwhelm a person, causing him to become easily confused and unable to think clearly. As a result, it becomes increasingly difficult for him to make accurate judgements and conclusions. To survive and emerge as the wisest, the individual must develop strategies to quiet his feelings of anxiety and keep them in a range where they benefit rather than harming him.

Anger and Frustration

When a person's attempts to achieve an objective are repeatedly hindered, he becomes frustrated. I can't help but imagine the feelings of those who came out every six years to compete against the mayor. Win or lose, the campaigns and associated work consume the same amount of time, money, energy, and other resources.

To survive, you must stay alive until help arrives. The person must do some chores with few resources to reach this aim. When attempting to complete these duties, it is unavoidable that something will go wrong; that something will occur outside of the survivor's control; and that, with one's life on the line, every mistake is magnified in terms of its significance. As a result, sooner or later, some will fail and survivors will emerge.

In a survival situation, numerous situations can annoy or infuriate a person. The weather, harsh terrain, hostile patrols, and physical limits are only a few sources of dissatisfaction and rage. Frustration and fury drive rash reactions, irrational behaviour, hasty decisions, and, in some cases, an "I quit" attitude (people sometimes avoid accomplishing those things they don't already know precisely how to do). If a person can control and channel the emotional intensity connected with rage and irritation, he can respond to survival obstacles in a useful manner. If the person's angry feelings aren't appropriately channelled, he can squander a lot of energy on actions that don't help his or others' prospects of survival.

The same conditions apply to those in a political race. If you're running against an incumbent who is hellbent on having his way despite widespread opposition, it'll only be a matter of time until you defeat him. As long as the people are the unifying stakeholder in democracy, whoever appeals to them the most will always emerge as the smartest in an ideal situation.

Likewise, politicians can use this to their advantage to sway voters to their side. Despite not being a typical politician, Martin Luther King Jr., the clever and skilled preacher, exhibited considerable political prowess in his time. He recognised when people were fearful, nervous, angry, or frustrated. All he had to do was tell them what they wanted to hear in his mellifluous voice powerfully and seductively. It's evident in every one of his speeches. His emotional intelligence was exceptional, and when combined with his zealous oratorical ability, he drew the attention of his country's leaders and that of many others around the world. Almost none of his words can be thrown away. In one of his legendary speeches, he said something so inspiring that the audience became enthralled and unstoppable in pursuing their goal. On August 28, 1963, in front of Lincoln's Memorial in Washington D.C., Martin Luther King delivered his most famous speech, "I Have A Dream." An enthralling excerpt from the speech goes thus:

"So, we have come here today to dramatise a shameful condition. In a sense, we have come to our nation's Capital to cash a check. When the architects of our great republic wrote the magnificent words of the Constitution and the Declaration of Independence, they were signing a promissory note to which every American was to fall heir.

This note was a promise that all men, yes, black men as well as white men, would be guaranteed the unalienable rights of life, liberty, and the pursuit of happiness. It is obvious today that America has defaulted on this promissory note insofar as her citizens of colour are concerned. Instead of honouring this sacred obligation, America has given its colored people a bad check, a check that has come back marked "insufficient funds."

But we refuse to believe that the bank of justice is bankrupt. We refuse to believe that there are insufficient funds in the great vaults of opportunity of this nation. So, we have come to cash this check, a check that will give us upon demand the riches of freedom and security of justice. We have also come to this hallowed spot to remind America of the fierce urgency of now. This is not time to engage in the luxury of cooling off or to take the tranquilising drug of gradualism. Now is the time to make real the promise of democracy."

Martin Luther King knew just what an enraged spirit needed to hear, and he led them by example and sacrifice. This can be seen in most of his talks, including the last speech he gave the evening before being assassinated.

"We've got some difficult days ahead," Martin Luther King, Jr., told an overflowing crowd in Memphis, Tennessee, on April 3, 1968, where the city's sanitation workers were striking. "But it really doesn't matter with me now because I've been to the mountaintop... I've seen the Promised Land. I may not get there with you. But I want you to know tonight, that we, as a people, will get to the Promised Land" (King, "I've Been," 222–223). Less than 24-hours after these prophetic words were spoken, King was assassinated by James Earl Ray.

Just like the King, when we were campaigning in the subsequent elections after the first, these were the points we kept hammering. Obama said, "Yes, we can," and we said,

"Togetherness." Together we can reach the promised land. Together we can arrive at our safe end. It always works. We reiterate until every fearful, angry, and frustrated soul becomes pacified and tranquil.

But, above and beyond tactics, we were always prepared to produce, and we did so despite all odds. Against all odds, the work becomes easier once you have people's best interests at heart and they have yours.

Depression

It is a rare person who does not feel melancholy, at least briefly, when faced with the rigours of survival. The competition becomes dismal and pressing over time. When this dissatisfaction worsens, we call it "depression." Depression is intricately tied to frustration and wrath. The frustrated guy becomes increasingly irritated as he fails to fulfil his goals. If the person's rage does not help them succeed, they will become even more frustrated.

The person is worn out physically, emotionally, and mentally due to a toxic cycle of wrath and frustration. When a person reaches this moment, he begins to give up, and his attention turns from "What can I do?" to "There is nothing I can do." Depression is a feeling of hopelessness and helplessness. There's nothing wrong with being sad for a moment when you remember your loved ones and what life is like in "civilization" or "the world." Such thoughts can motivate you to put in more effort and live another day. On the other side, allowing oneself to get depressed can drain your vitality and, more importantly, your will to live.

Loneliness

Humans are social animals. We like being in the company of other humans. "Never go alone in a group," I noted in the playbook I supplied in the first chapter. "A wingman/wingwoman is always present with a winner." However, if your wingperson goes silent one day, you can position yourself in reverse order at the other end. Few people who began their careers with the mayor have remained with him; politics remains politics.

Using the Russian President as a political example, I will try to convey the strength of this instinct. Vladimir Putin is one of the most well-known leaders who has mastered these tendencies, exhibiting how you may be purposefully alone while also being a "people person" as often as the situation requires. Putin's biography portrays a man of modest ambition and humble beginnings: clever, competent, and loyal; an organiser and team player. He is a populist in the sense that he understands and speaks the language of common people, but he is also a bureaucrat and a functionary. His perspective is based on two poles: state service and care for the common people. Two different things demanding their opposite selves almost simultaneously. He must stay alone to have quality time to reason as the number one citizen in Russia, but he must talk to his people to be seen and felt by his citizens as their leader

Putin was a product of the Soviet Union and a devout follower of its policies. He was, likewise, a product of the Yeltsin regime and a devoted follower. Putin appears to be more at ease in post-1991 Russia than in the USSR before 1991, based on his personality and public pronouncements. He is the first post-Soviet leader, a man who knows how to live in the "New Russia," with its advantages and disadvantages. Both the "closet liberal" and "closet authoritarian" interpretations can be found in his life narrative. He served in the KGB for sixteen years, but he was instrumental in bringing capitalism to Petersburg. He was the first Russian leader since Lenin to speak a foreign language and reside outside of Russia, though he did so in East Germany as a KGB agent.

Also indisputable is that his biography provided the raw material to fashion a political persona that Russian voters found powerfully attractive. Note that Putin rose through patronage and not by competing in elections or working inside a political party. He was selected as a trustworthy aide by officials at ever-higher levels of responsibility. Patron-client relations were central to cadre policy in the Soviet era. They paradoxically became even more dominant as a vehicle for elite recruitment during the Yeltsin years, when Russia was becoming a democracy. This was true even for the teams of liberal reformers led by Anatolii Chubais and Boris Nemtsov, which were recruited through patronage networks.

Putin's tactics to undermine democratic institutions worldwide were developed at 'home,' and he has used them against the Russian people with increasing impunity over nearly two decades. As a result, hundreds of billions of dollars have been stolen and syphoned off to foreign shores, all while independent media and civil society, elections, political parties, and cultural institutions have been manipulated and suppressed, putting a significant dent in the ability of domestic opponents to effectively challenge Putin's regime.

While he was consolidating his hold on power at home, Mr. Putin oversaw an opportunistic expansion of malign influence operations abroad, which targeted vulnerable states on Russia's periphery as well as countries affiliated with Western institutions such as the European Union (EU) and North Atlantic Treaty Organisation (NATO). Putin's administration has significantly increased its investments in propaganda outlets outside of Russia's borders, funded and supported non-governmental organisations and political parties that advance Mr. Putin's anti-European Union and anti-NATO agenda, nationalised mafia groups to assist the state in money laundering and other criminal activities abroad, and used its near-monopoly over energy supplies in some countries to exert influence and spread corruption.

That Putin is ultimately in charge and capable of making extremely important decisions on his own in an environment of complete secrecy is demonstrated in this instance. Putin very often consults with no one, and when he does, it is done in a completely opaque manner. He's not one to be overt about his feelings. Even if he consults with a few people in his circle, they leave without a clear understanding of what he is trying to accomplish and are forced to guess. They are sometimes correct in their predictions, making educated guesses at times. Sometimes they try to curry favour and are successful, and other times they are unsuccessful. He ultimately has the final say in all matters of policy. The strategy and grand plans he has for Russia, in their entirety, are only concepts in his imagination.

More recently (and most likely as a result of his invasion of Ukraine), every Putin move has been scrutinised as a mixture of feelings of patriotism and fear escalate among the Russian people and the rest of the world—particularly among Ukrainians. Putin sits or stands at a distance from every world leader who has ever spoken with him in the recent past, which has piqued observers' interest. The reason why Putin chooses to sit across from a ridiculously large table during meetings with other world leaders, the most recent example being a meeting with German Chancellor Olaf Scholz, is unclear.

Following a meeting in Moscow in which Putin and French President Emmanuel Macron were seated at opposite ends of a table estimated to be twenty feet long, the issue gained international attention for the first time. According to reports, Macron refused to submit to a Covid-19 PCR test administered by a Russian doctor, which resulted in extreme social distance.

French President Emmanuel Macron (R) meets with Russian President Vladimir Putin (L) in Moscow Source: SPUTNIK/ AFP VIA GETTY IMAGES

However, President Putin even keeps his aides at a significant distance from him. During a one-on-one meeting with the president, Russian Foreign Minister Sergey Lavrov sat at the other end of a different, extremely long table from the president. According to what I witnessed, the table at his meeting with this minister was significantly longer than the table at his previous encounters with presidents and other world leaders. These are all indications that the president understands the importance of not having his head covered and that he would never admit to readily because he is such a wittily intelligent individual.

Russian President Vladimir Putin (R) and Foreign Minister Sergei Lavrov hold a meeting Source: SPUTNIK/AFP VIA GETTY IMAGES

Of course, many people are convinced of the genius with which Russia's strongman president manipulates the situation. However, a politician with Putin's ability to deceive both his own people and the rest of the world is a dangerous prospect.

Even though many of our world-class politicians were blind to the authoritarian face of the real Putin, many of his own people were also not able to see behind the curtain and recognise him for what he truly was.

Being alone all of the time is not something most people enjoy! Being in a survival situation comes with significant risks of isolation, as you are aware, and aspiring to a political position is nothing more than a survival situation in and of its own. This isn't too bad, though. Loneliness and boredom can bring to the surface abilities you previously believed were only possessed by other people. If you're like most people, you'll be surprised at how far your imagination and ingenuity can take you. When you are forced to do something, you may discover hidden talents and abilities. But, perhaps most importantly, you may find a level of inner strength and tenacity of which you were previously unaware. On the other hand, feelings of loneliness and boredom can be depressing. Whether you are living alone or with others, you must develop techniques to keep your mind active and engaged. Furthermore, you must achieve a certain level of self-sufficiency. You must have confidence in your abilities if you are to "go it alone." However, I do not believe it must be in the same vein as Putin's.

Guilt

The circumstances leading to your being in a survival setting are sometimes dramatic and tragic. It may result from an accident or military mission where there was a loss of life. Perhaps you were the only, or one of a few, survivors. While naturally relieved to be alive, you simultaneously may be mourning the deaths of others who were less fortunate. It is not uncommon for survivors to feel guilty about being spared from death while others were not. When used positively, this feeling has encouraged people to try harder to survive with the belief they were allowed to live for some greater purpose in life. Sometimes, survivors tried to stay alive to carry on the work of those killed. Whatever reason you give yourself, do not let feelings of guilt prevent you from living. The living who abandon their chance to survive accomplish nothing. Such an act would be the greatest tragedy.

✶✶✶✶✶✶✶✶✶✶

Let me now construct a picture of human nature and instincts based on some more intellectual comparisons. Graham Wallas' book "Human Nature In Politics" is a popular psychology book from long ago. I'll quote from the third edition of 1920, which was included in Constable's Miscellany of Original & Selected Publications in Literature 1929. Wallas did an excellent job of intellectually studying human nature as it impacts and relates to politics. "Impulse and instinct in politics" was the opening chapter, and it was from this chapter I grafted the comparisons that follow.

According to Wallas, an investor, for example, wants solid security mixed with 5% interest. He spends an hour reviewing the price list of stocks with an open mind and concludes that purchasing Brewery Debentures will allow him to fully realise his objective. Given his initial desire for good security, his purchase of the Debentures looks to be the logical conclusion of his reasoning. The desire for decent security may also appear to be only an intellectual conclusion about how to satisfy some greater universal desire, shared by all humanity, for 'pleasure,' our own 'interest,' or anything similar. The satisfaction of this general desire can then be treated as the supreme 'end' of life, from which all our acts and impulses, great and small, are derived by the same intellectual process as that by which the conclusion is derived from the premises of an argument.

Common sense is a term used to describe this method of thinking. A passage from Macaulay's famous attack on Bentham's Utilitarian followers in the Edinburgh Review of March 1829 is a fine example of its application to politics. Jeremy Bentham was a philosopher, economist, jurist, and legal reformer who founded modern utilitarianism. This ethical theory holds that actions are morally right if they tend to promote happiness or pleasure among all those affected by them (and morally wrong if they tend to encourage unhappiness or pain).

From the work of Bentham, Macauley quoted, "It is totally impossible to deduce the science of governance from the principles of human nature," according to this extreme example of the foundation of politics on dogmatic psychology. "Is there any notion about human nature that is completely and universally true?" Macaulay wonders. "There is just one that we are aware of, and it is that men always act in their own self-interest. When we witness a man's conduct, we can tell exactly what he thinks his interests are." Macaulay believes he is battling Benthamism from root to branch. Still, he is subconsciously accepting and exaggerating the assumption held by Bentham and most other eighteenth and early nineteenth-century philosophers: that all reasons arise from the idea of a planned purpose.

If he had been pressed, Macaulay would probably have admitted that there are cases in which human acts and impulses to act occur independently of any idea of an end to be gained by them. If I have a piece of grit in my eye and ask someone to take it out with the corner of his handkerchief, I generally close the eye as soon as the cloth comes near and always feel a strong impulse to do so. Nobody supposes that I close my eyes because, after due consideration, I think it is in my best interest to do so. Nor do most men choose to run away in battle, fall in love, vote a candidate or not, or talk about the weather to satisfy their desire for a preconceived end.

If a man were followed through one ordinary day without his knowing it by a camera, and all his acts and words were reproduced before him the next day, he would be astonished to find how few of them were the result of a deliberate search for the means of attaining ends. He would, of course, see that much of his activity consisted in the half-conscious repetition, under the influence of habit, of movements that were originally more fully conscious. But even if all cases of habit were excluded, he would find that only a small proportion of the residue could be explained as being directly produced by an intellectual calculation. If a record were also kept of his impulses and emotions which did not result in action, it would be realized that they were the same kind as those which did. Very few of them would have been preceded by that process Macaulay takes for granted.

Macaulay might even have admitted that the mental act of calculation is preceded by an impulse to calculate, which impulse may have nothing to do with any prior consideration of means and ends and may range from the half-conscious yielding to a train of reverie to the obstinate driving of a tired brain onto the difficult task of precise thought.

Every psychology student is now warned about the "intellectualist" mistake, as is shown by my Macaulay quotation. It is now widely accepted that impulse has its own evolutionary history separate from the history of the cognitive processes via which it is frequently directed and modified. Because such reactions have been effective in the past in perpetuating our species, our inherited organisation incentivizes us to react in specific ways to certain stimuli.

We couldn't keep winning if that weren't the case; it's what the people want, even if they don't realise it. We boosted human nature's natural willingness and tendencies. Some of the reactions we're discussing are 'instincts,' or urges toward specific acts or series of behaviours, regardless of any conscious prediction of their likely consequences. Those instincts are sometimes unconscious and involuntary, and sometimes conscious and intentional, as they appear to be in humans and other higher animals. However, the relationship between means and ends that they display is the product of the 'fittest' of many different dispositions to act in surviving in the past, not of any contrivance by the actor. Indeed, the instinct remains even when it is pointless, such as when a dog circles around to flatten the grass before settling down on a carpet, and even when it is deadly, such as when a typhoid patient craves solid food.

We usually think of 'instinct' as a collection of discrete inclinations, each pointing to a specific deed or series of acts.

However, there is no reason to believe that the entire body of inherited impulses has ever been divided in this way, even among non-human species. The evolution of impulse must have been a long and winding road. In addition to impulses toward specific acts, we can detect vague and generalised tendencies in all animals, often overlapping and contradictory, such as curiosity and shyness, sympathy and cruelty, imitation and restless activity—all of which may have survived with modifications because it produced a different result. It is thus possible to avoid Mr. Balfour's ingenious dilemma, according to which we must either demonstrate that the desire for scientific truth, for example, is lineally descended from one of the specific instincts that teach us 'to fight, to eat, and to bring up children,' or accept the supernatural authority of the Shorter Catechism.

The pre-rational nature of many of our impulses is obscured, however, by the fact that they are increasingly transformed by memory, habit, and cognition over the course of a person's lifespan. Through imitation or habits, nonhuman creatures can adapt and adjust their innate impulses based on personal experience. When telegraph lines were initially installed, many birds flew into them and were killed. Although the number of dead birds was insufficient to cause a change in the species' biological inheritance, very few birds now fly against the wires. The young birds must have mimicked their elders, who had learned to avoid the wires, in the same way as many hunting animals' offspring are believed to learn gadgets and precautions as a result of their parents' experience. They then build and pass down imitation creations of their own.

Many directly inherited impulses appear in man and other animals at a certain point in their development, then die away if checked or form habits if they are unchecked. Impulses that were once strong and useful may no longer help preserve life and may be weakened by biological degeneration, as the whale's legs or our teeth and hair are. Such transient or weaker impulses are particularly susceptible to being transferred to new objects or altered by experience and thought.

The schoolmaster must cope with all of these intricate realities. In Macaulay's day, he was directed by his 'common sense,' and the entire process was intellectualised. The poor lads who acted on an ancient urge to fidget, play truant, chase cats, or imitate their teacher were questioned and met with repeated threats of punishment. They were compelled to concoct some far-fetched fiction, and they were punished for it due to their ignorance of their own evolutionary history.

The trained schoolmaster of today accepts the existence of such impulses as a given and decides how far he will check them in each case by relying on the half-conscious imitation that makes up the majority of classroom discipline, and how far he will stimulate a conscious recognition of the ethical or penal connection between acts and their consequences. In any event, his ability to manage instinctive impulses stems from his understanding of its non-intellectual source. He could even apply this knowledge to his own impulses, overcoming the belief that his aggravation during afternoon school in July is the product of an intellectual conclusion about the necessity for extra vigilance in dealing with a group of unusually bad lads.

On the other hand, the politician is still as prone to intellectualise impulses as the schoolmaster was fifty years ago. He has two excuses: he deals exclusively with adults, whose impulses are more deeply influenced by experience and thought than those of children, and it is extremely difficult for anyone thinking about politics not to limit his consideration to those political actions and impulses that are accompanied by the most conscious thought, and thus enter his mind first. But the politician thinks about men in large communities, and it is in forecasting the action of large communities that the intellectualist fallacy is most misleading. The results of experience and thought are often confined to individuals or small groups, and when they differ may cancel each other as political forces. The original human impulses are, with personal variations, common to the whole race and increase in their importance with an increase in the number of those influenced by them.

It might be worthwhile to attempt a description of some of the more obvious or important political impulses, keeping in mind that, unlike children and animals, we are dealing with tendencies that have been weakened by human evolution, are more often transferred to new uses, and act not simply but in combination or counteraction.

For example, Aristotle claims that "Affection' (or 'friendship,' since the meaning of 'ριλ•α' lies halfway between the two terms) is what makes political union possible," and that it is "what law-givers deem more important than justice." It's a hereditary inclination among creatures of the same race, especially among men. If we look for political attachment in its most basic form, we can find it in our need to feel "kindly" toward every other human being whose existence and personality we become acutely aware of. Others can check and override this impulse, but anyone can test its existence and pre-rationality in their own case by going to the British Museum and seeing how the discovery that a little Egyptian girl baby who died four thousand years ago rubbed the toes of her shoes bare by crawling on the floor affects his feelings.

The majority of techniques used in an election are contrivances designed to generate this fleeting feeling of personal dedication. The candidate is advised to "show himself constantly," "give away prizes," and "say a few words" at the end of other people's speeches—all in situations where there is little or no opportunity for those present to form a reasoned opinion of his merits, but plenty of opportunities to develop a purely instinctive affection for him. A good, distinctive likeness is more successful than a pleasing snapshot in his portrait, which is distributed daily. The best of all is a snapshot of him in his yard, smoking a pipe, or reading a newspaper, which brings his everyday reality to life.

A simple-minded supporter who has become overly enamoured will try to rationalise their feelings. He'll say that the man, about whom he knows nothing except that he was photographed wearing a Panama hat and holding a fox-terrier, is 'the kind of man we want,' and he's decided to support him. It is similar to a child who will say that he loves his mother because she's the best mother in the world, or to a man in love who offers an elaborate explanation of his perfectly normal feelings, which he describes as an intellectual inference from alleged abnormal excellence. In the same way, the applicant instinctively intellectualises. One of the most self-effacing individuals I know once told me that he was 'going around' among his future constituents 'to show them what a nice guy I am.' Many men find the procedure incomprehensible until it can be intellectualised.

We know a king is a life-long candidate in the case of born leaders, and there is a remarkably intricate traditional skill of building personal affection for him. It is more vital for him to be seen than it is for him to speak or act. His face appears on every coin and stamp, and it has the most significant impact when it is a good likeness, regardless of personal beauty. If you are an avaricious reader of past events, you may recall how people realized how their emotions shifted during the later years of Queen Victoria's reign. People were said to have remembered a measurable increase in their affection for her when, in 1897, a thoroughly life-like portrait was imprinted on the nation's coins.

In the case of a monarchy, one can also see how media, official biographers, courtiers, and possibly the monarch himself intellectualise the entire process. The more ordinary the occurrences reported are, the more likely they are to establish a clear sense of his personality and produce this particular feeling. For example, reports in the daily bulletin of data about his walks and drives are particularly beneficial. However, because a feeling coming from ordinary circumstances is difficult to explain solely intellectually, these events indicate a life of incredible regularity and industry. When love is formed, it is frequently portrayed as an unavoidable reasoned conclusion emerging from contemplation on a reign marked by an unusually high number of good harvests or brilliant inventions.

Let me return to the subject of dread for a moment. Fear frequently accompanies and is confused with fondness in politics. Unintentionally, a guy whose lifelong ambition has been to see and speak with his king is brought face to face with him. Because any sudden movement might have revealed his ancestors to a lion or a bear, or even earlier, to a hungry cuttlefish, he becomes 'stuck to the place,' pales, and is unable to speak.

It would be an interesting experiment if a professor of experimental psychology arranged his class in the laboratory with sphygmographs on their wrists set up to record pulse movements that accompany the sensation of 'thrill.' He would then introduce a bishop, a well-known general, the greatest living man of letters, and a minor member of the royal family into the room without notice and in random order. The resulting records of immediate pulse disturbances would be extremely valuable scientifically. It might even be possible to keep the record going for a quarter of a minute in each case, tracing the secondary effects of differences in political opinions, education, or humour among the students.

A thorough book on political impulses would include the fighting instinct (and the role it plays, along with affection and loyalty, in the formation of parties) and the instincts of mistrust, curiosity, and the desire to excel. These primary impulses have a much greater immediate effect when they are 'pure,' that is, when they are not accompanied by competing or opposing impulses. This is the main reason art, which aims to produce one emotion at a time, acts on most men so much more easily than real life's more varied appeal.

So far, I've focused on the impulses exemplified by a modern state's internal politics. But probably the most essential element of the entire psychology of political impulse is that which deals with racial impulses that manifest themselves in international politics, rather than the emotional effect of inhabitants of any state on one other. The world's future peace is primarily determined by whether we have, as is sometimes claimed and supposed, an intuitive affinity for human beings with similar looks and colours to our own and an instinctual dislike for those who are unlike us.

According to psychologists, it is difficult to dogmatise on this subject without a thorough assessment of the facts. But I'm inclined to believe that the intense and seemingly simple cases of racial hatred and devotion that can be found are the product of multiple different and comparably weak impulses coupled and heightened by habit and connection, rather than a single and universal inclination.

The relationship between man's nature and the environment into which he is born determines his impulses, thoughts, and actions. This chapter looked at the relationship from the perspective of man's nature (insofar as it influences politics). So, in the following part, I will dive deeper into the campaign strategies and tactics you've long been awaiting.

Chapter Three

Political Marketing

Political marketing is an essential component of political life. Presidents and prime ministers, politicians and political parties, government departments, and councils all use marketing to achieve their political objectives. When deciding on policies and service design, market research is used to understand what the people they serve and seek votes from want and need. Voter profiling assists in the creation of new segments to target. Strategy guides the creation of the political brand to develop an appealing vision. Internal marketing guides the provision of volunteer involvement. Analytics and experimental research test and refines communication and messages. And delivery management sets expectations and assists in the delivery of services.

Political marketing is a modern and dynamic field of academic research and teaching that seeks to understand, learn from, comment on, and even influence such behaviour. Political marketing also piques the public's interest and sparks debate. Many recent films, including Game Change, The Iron Lady, The Ides of March, and No; and TV shows, including The West Wing, VEEP, and Scandal, have focused on strategy, branding, positioning, crisis management, and polling, as well as ethical issues of authenticity, targeting ethnic minorities, and gender.

Political parties around the world are learning that to compete with rival parties, they must invest in digital marketing in addition to traditional mediums such as television and newspapers. In recent years, we've seen an increase in U.K. and U.S. political parties, in particular, using social media campaigns to defeat their opponents.

This chapter explores the evolution of political marketing strategy and looks back at some key marketing elements of prominent past campaigns worldwide.

So, What Is Political Marketing?

I'm sure I'll give many contextual definitions of this term before I finish this chapter and the book as a whole, but there's one in particular I'd like to mention right now... Marketing in the 21st century is based on digital marketing.

Political marketing can be defined as *"the application of marketing principles and procedures in political campaigns by various individuals and organisations. The procedures involved include the analysis, development, execution, and management of strategic campaigns by candidates, political parties, governments, lobbyists and interest groups that seek to drive public opinion, advance their own ideologies, win elections, and pass legislation and referenda in response to the needs and wants of selected people and groups in a society"* (Newman, 1999, p. xiii).

A Brief History of Marketing in Politics

In the past, America was somewhat ahead of many other nations when it came to political marketing. This is most likely due to the emergence of the Internet, which was domiciled in their part of the world ahead of others. Stanley Kelley, an American, is widely credited with coining the term "political marketing" in 1956. In the United States, John Beckley, a member of Thomas Jefferson's campaign team, is cited as one of the first political consultants. However, similar roles were undoubtedly identified much earlier in other societies. Political marketing has grown in popularity in recent years due to the growth of an investigative press, declining party loyalty, and changes in the political and electoral systems.

Scholars have identified media expansion, particularly television, as having had a significant impact. There is evidence that political marketing has aided in improving communication between politicians and voters. The obsession with image and how much or little it affects the voter is especially visible in popular and academic literature on political marketing and political communication. The phenomenon of image in politics is frequently attributed to television.

However, the word 'image' has nearly as many meanings as the number of people who use it. In terms of political marketing, concepts from consumer behaviour and political science were combined to create a voting behaviour model. It has, thus far, only been tested in a primary election in the United States, and its applicability outside of such settings has yet to be demonstrated. The majority of the literature focuses on what marketers would consider tactical issues, but Butler and Collins (1996) demonstrate the impact of strategy and its importance in governing the campaign's direction. Most Western electoral markets are mature, with well-established players and positions.

As early as the nineteenth century, politicians used newspaper advertisements to raise voter awareness. Marketing strategies have evolved in tandem with technological advancements. Radio advertisements resulted from the invention of radio, whereas television advertisements resulted from the invention of television. In 1952, Dwight Eisenhower ran for the American presidency, becoming the first presidential candidate to run solely on television marketing and promotion.

The first mass media campaign was launched in 1960, during the election of John F. Kennedy vs. Richard Nixon. Until then, mass media had only been used by companies competing for sales of consumer goods. According to Bruce Newman, this was the beginning of the modernization of marketing in a political context. Political strategists began to follow Wall Street's lead. Politicians quickly learned to 'brand' themselves as branding and positioning became more critical in marketing consumer products. Reagan was among the first to actively employ this strategy, ensuring that he stood in front of an American flag whenever he appeared on stage during his 1980 campaign.

The 1988 election between George Bush, Sr. and Michael Dukakis was a watershed moment in American politics because it was the first to employ negative campaigning. To make negative statements about Dukakis, Bush used a strategy known as "positioning yourself via re-positioning your competition."

Through this methodology, statements were made to make himself look better by emphasising his opponent's flaws rather than his own. Bill Clinton's presidential campaign headquarters were well-known for their "war room," a high-tech nerve centre that integrated data into strategy development. From a marketing standpoint, the goal of this war room was to turn Bill Clinton into a service that the Democratic Party could "sell."

Political Propaganda

Propaganda is the spread of information—facts, arguments, rumours, half-truths, or lies—in order to influence public opinion. Propaganda is distinguished from casual conversation or the free and easy exchange of ideas by its deliberateness and a heavy emphasis on manipulation. Propaganda is, more or less, the systematic use of symbols to influence other people's beliefs, attitudes, or actions—including words, gestures, banners, monuments, music, clothing, insignia, hairstyles, designs on coins and postage stamps, and so forth. Propagandists work toward a specific goal or set of goals. They carefully select facts, arguments, and symbol displays to accomplish this, presenting them in ways they believe will have the most significant impact. They may omit or distort pertinent facts or simply lie to maximize the effect. They may also try to divert the reactors' (the people they are attempting to sway) attention away from everything except their own propaganda.

Propaganda has become more common in political contexts, specifically to refer to particular efforts sponsored by governments and political groups and frequently covert interests.

Propaganda was exemplified in the early twentieth century by party slogans. Until the first half of the twentieth century, political propaganda was limited to the mass dissemination of arbitrary ideas. In fact, the term propaganda—derived from the Latin "propagare," which means "to spread, to extend, to be disclosed"—has historically been regarded as a synonym for exaggeration, misrepresentation, and abuse in connection with the launch of a series of messages aimed at influencing citizens' value systems and behaviours.

An example of propaganda proliferation can, once again, be seen in Putin-led Russia. We previously discussed Putin's clamp-down on the free press, social media, and freedom of speech. In Russia, the government controls the entire narrative, so it is easy to be brainwashed. The Russian people, many of whom have never heard the other side of the story, believe the rhetoric without questioning it because their media has been so inundated with propaganda. They are bombarded with one-sided information, so they do not have the tools to critically assess the stream of information. Hence, they are swayed by the propaganda to believe their side is right and blindly follow their charismatic leader, even if all the facts tell a different story and point to a false-flag operation. It is easier than one might believe to be brainwashed by one side or the other.

On the other hand, political marketing has generally become a more positive term as it has emerged as a new and independent branch of political science within the contemporary realm of democratic values. It is concerned with the dissemination of a message and gaining extensive knowledge of the democratic "game"—that is, how to avoid abusive and illegal practices that may be used by or against you in the future. Furthermore, since its inception, political marketing has engaged in critical dialogues with an increasing number of fields, including pure statistics, development studies, game theory, corporate ethics, crowd psychology, and so on, successfully cultivating its own theoretical framework and identity as a distinct science.

The distinction between propaganda and political marketing became more evident in the 1950s. If propaganda was heavily based on personal charisma, the then-presidential candidate General Dwight Eisenhower decided to hire the advertising agency BBDO (Barton, Durstine, Osborn & Batten Co.) to work on his image during the election campaign in 1952. At this point, the candidate began to be regarded as a political agent for social transformation (a political product) rather than simply as a charismatic individual. The role of BBDO was to change Eisenhower's image from that of a wartime general to that of an efficient administrator.

Furthermore, BBDO was tasked with adapting the candidate's language for radio and television inserts. These two communication channels were beginning to play a decisive role in American (and global) presidential campaigns. From this point forward, the history of modern political marketing took on a new, solid form, becoming the conduit to very well-structured electoral campaigns with the strategic support of mass communication media. At first, this was TV and radio, until the arrival of more modern vehicles that would forever change the reality of political marketing: the Internet and social networks.

Mainstream Marketing vs. Political Marketing

Marketing itself is a form of management approach used primarily by business organisations. It has evolved to include the design and promotion of a product to ensure that the organisation's goals are met, the primary one being profit in the case of a business. Marketing is more than just selling or, in political parlance, campaigning. The distinction between marketing and selling is more than merely semantic. Selling is concerned with the needs of the seller, whereas marketing is concerned with the needs of the buyer. Selling is preoccupied with the seller's need to convert his product into cash; marketing is preoccupied with the idea of satisfying the customer's needs through the product and everything associated with creating, delivering, and finally consuming it. The current marketing philosophy focuses on how firms can satisfy customers and adopts what is known as market orientation, as this is deemed the most effective way for firms to meet their goals. Customers are more likely to buy a product if the company provides what they want and the company profits.

There are some distinctions between political marketing and mainstream marketing practises, which include the following:

1. Unlike any other purchase, all voters make their decision on the same day. Furthermore, while opinion polls and brand share tracking methods are similar, the latter is based on actual purchasing decisions, whereas the former is based on hypothetical questions.

2. Unlike any other purchase decision, voting has no direct or indirect individual costs associated with it.

3. Voters must accept the collective choice, even if it is not their preferred option.

4. In elections, the winner takes all, especially in countries where the electoral system is "first past the post," as in the United Kingdom.

5. Political parties and candidates are complex intangible products that voters cannot unbundle, so they must decide on the entire package.

6. It is extremely difficult in many countries to form a new and successful political party solely through marketing.

7. Brand leaders tend to stay in front in most mainstream marketing situations.

8. Unlike the commercial world, the political arena is fraught with ideas, emotions, conflict, and partisanship.

9. Negative advertising is not permitted in mainstream marketing.

The Relationship Between Digital Marketing and Politics

Clearly, the Internet has changed how political campaigns and marketing are conducted. Campaigns must now maintain a digital presence for their candidate, and they have a plethora of new channels through which to distribute messaging and communicate with voters.

From what we've been saying, you would've deduced that as it is, marketing and politics are inextricably linked. Marketing has a variety of brilliant definitions, but I want to adapt a particular definition to this context. According to Merriam-Webster, marketing is the process of making people aware of a product. In our case, which is politics, the candidate is the product. Voters must be able to picture a candidate as an officer in the position for which he is running.

Political marketing methods are at an all-time high whenever an election approaches. For example, President Barack Obama's victory in America demonstrated that political marketing is critical to the success of a presidential campaign; however, I would argue that any election, not just presidential elections, could benefit from marketing. Both of Obama's presidential campaigns are considered master classes in election digital marketing. He used the Internet to reach previously unengaged voting blocs in an unprecedented way.

Obama raised the bar, and in the elections that followed, it was raised farther. President Trump's election was very heavily reliant on a robust social media presence, through which he connected with disenfranchised voters. In this way, (and perhaps through nefarious methods discussed below) he created a platform which was at times controversial, but highly effective in garnering the support of his target demographic.

In an open and transparent modern political competition, contestants require a method for distributing political products to the public, such as new ideas, issues, party ideology, programmes, and leadership characteristics. To win the election, they must be able to implement new political communication strategies that are more oriented toward voters and understand how this can be done by utilizing marketing strategies to promote the candidate and their political values. The use of political marketing, on the other hand, has an impact on the health of democracy. Some academics believe that it benefits the democratic system. Despite these positive effects, political marketing has some drawbacks.

To illustrate what I am saying, take the Cambridge Analytical and Facebook saga, for example. A massive data breach was discovered in early 2018 involving Facebook and Cambridge Analytica, a political data analytics firm. The uncanny saga is even the subject of a film titled "The Great Hack." The epic movie explained thoroughly how the political data analytics firm inappropriately stole personal data from over 87 million Facebook users. Other popular social media sites were utilised in addition to Facebook. Here, we're talking about specialists. In an internal business document obtained by the Guardian, the plan for how Cambridge Analytica claimed to have won the White House for Donald Trump by utilising Google, Snapchat, Twitter, Facebook, and YouTube is disclosed for the first time. Following the publication of this news, Facebook came under fire from lawmakers in the United States and the United Kingdom. Trump, on the other hand, was already inextricably the President of the United States.

At this point, I should mention that much of the candidates' success in winning votes is dependent on how well their campaigns are run and the impact of their political marketing strategy. When an election is in full swing, citizens are focused on determining who will receive their vote. Without a doubt, the issues continue to play a significant role in political campaigns. The image of the candidate, on the other hand, is critical. Voters must be able to envision a candidate serving as an officer in the position for which he is running. This is where political marketing strategy comes into play. General election campaigns make use of a variety of techniques.

Public Outreach

The Internet offers easy and efficient methods to reach the general public quickly. This especially comes in handy with fundraising and grassroots organising. Information about supporters can be found online, helping political campaigns engage volunteers and solicit donations.

Obama's commitment to digital outreach fuelled an extensive grassroots campaign that used the Internet to organise, even in places where there was little physical campaign presence. Supporters called voters from their personal computers. They revolutionised email campaigning and came up with the "Click to Donate" button.

Digital Branding

The Internet also provides unique ways for candidates to develop their personal brands and platforms. Websites allow for in-depth descriptions of views and issues. Social media offers an easy way to share content for wide distribution. With so many opportunities to spread the word, candidates can build a brand voters will identify with.

In 2008, Obama created a digital brand based on his message of change. This simple message and his narrative of being a political outsider truly resonated with the general public.

Obama used digital media to share the story on his own terms and reached voters who were previously unengaged. Obama registered massive numbers of young and minority voters.

Social Media

The emergence of social media has helped candidates reach more people and target them more precisely. Social media marketing allows candidates to spread their messages both broadly and quickly. It also offers the ability to develop extremely targeted advertising and messaging. Ads can be tailored to groups by age, location, and other demographics, which can go a long way toward establishing efficient social campaign teams.

According to Mashable, by the end of his second campaign, Obama's Facebook page had 34 million fans. Ninety-eight percent of American Facebook users were friends with an Obama fan. He also had 24 million Twitter followers, and his victory photo was his most retweeted tweet ever. Obama's social team targeted the 18- to 29-year-old demographic extensively via mobile advertising and urged supporters to spread the word.

The Use of Political Marketing

I want to talk purely about political marketing without relating it with any other thing here—just the term and its functions. Political marketing is a relatively new (but famous) field of study within the discipline of political science and communication that investigates the use of marketing techniques in the political process. However, it has piqued the interest of not only many academics (from management, communication, and political science) but also politicians, bureaucrats, and political professionals.

Political marketing is the use of marketing tools, techniques, and methods in the political process. In other words, political marketing is the result of marketing and politics combined. It reflects the activity and method of marketing's penetration of the political space. Popular methods in political marketing include political advertising, celebrity endorsements, the involvement of professional consultants and campaign managers, online campaigning, mobile phone canvassing, segmentation, and micro-targeting.

Professional marketing has had an impact on the working styles of political parties. Parties have become more market-oriented, framing their programmes and policies in response to polls and market surveys. The information revolution and globalisation have played critical roles in transforming traditional political campaigning into one of the most professional and sophisticated marketing tactics. It is argued that if a political party incorporates the marketing philosophy, it will seek to meet voters' needs and wants, resulting in voter satisfaction, thus gaining electoral support to meet its own goals (Marshment, 2006).

Before that, political marketing was thought to serve a unique purpose in achieving the goal of political activities through strategic planning, preparation, design, and packaging of political issues, which is the distribution of political information based on public segmentation. The ultimate goal is to create a mutually satisfying and harmonious state for both political parties and voters.

Marrek (1995:2) defines political marketing as "a complex process, the result of a larger effort involving all the factors of a politician's political communication" and emphasises that "political marketing" is the general method of "political communication." Political marketing, in his opinion, has become an essential component of political communication.

Furthermore, according to Ocass (1996:48), the use of marketing in political campaigns "provides political parties with the ability to address voter concerns and needs through marketing analysis, planning, implementation, and control of political and electoral campaigns." The primary goal of political marketing is to assist political parties and voters in making the most appropriate and satisfying decisions.

Many studies on the increased professionalisation of political marketing campaigns have been completed. These include the rise of the class of political consultants, pollsters, and advertising executives and the result of political parties and interest groups engaging in strategic communications (Norris, 2004:1).

Furthermore, the practice of political marketing can be distinguished by six characteristics. Today's political campaigns are primarily based on single issues and candidate centralism. Second, the importance of money, particularly in pre-nomination presidential campaigns, is growing due to media advertising. Third, the number of professional communicators who use effective, new communication technology is growing. Today's campaign strategies are carried out by public relations experts, fundraisers, and opinion pollsters. Fourth, the role of the media has grown because it is a very effective tool that enables candidates to be recognised and aids parties in evaluating their campaign performance. Fifth, the bond between citizens and political parties is deteriorating. Finally, there is growing concern about the consultants' influence and activities 2012:2 (Ugur).

Not surprisingly, the presence of marketing in politics is becoming increasingly important because political actors today (including not only political parties and politicians, but also governments, single-issue groups, lobbying organisations, and so on) not only act according to marketing principles, but also "think" in marketing terms when it comes to their political activities (Henneberg, 2004, p. 4). For example, using a candidate pair's name with two syllables is intended to be more easily recognised and popular in public memory while aiding the management of politicians' image and popularity. It is a form of marketing similar to developing and marketing a business product.

Political marketing applications have evolved from a communication tool to a coherent method of managing politics, whether policy formulation, election canvassing, or decision execution. However, most political actors lack a comprehensive and sophisticated understanding of marketing applications for situations involving political exchange. Political marketing management in politics has led to some "leading" parties and candidates adopting a simplistic and populist "follower mentality," contributing to electorate disenchantment and cynicism about politics.

Furthermore, political communication today is about building the political image of political institutions or politicians rather than transmitting political messages or values to the public. According to Simons (2006), "Contemporary democratic politics are frequently characterised as "image politics," in which style is more important than substance and personalities are more important than policies. Citizens and electorates are said to be "enslaved by political image."

As a result, the political image has become increasingly important in campaigns, particularly during elections. According to Newman (1999:88), one of the most powerful marketing tools a politician can use to influence public opinion is his or her image. Craig contends, in relation to the political image:

"The personal image of political leaders is a focus of contemporary political communication, but the looks, style, and character of politicians is only the most prominent product of a process in which a broad range of personnel deploy their sophisticated skills to produce political texts and images, control the flow of information within and across organisations, and manage relations with the mass media and the public (Craig, 2004:130)."

Functions of Political Marketing

Ensuring that each of the functions of political marketing are in place is a prerequisite for successful political marketing management. According to political marketing theory, there are eight generic functions of successful political marketing, including:

1. **Product Function:** In political marketing, there should be an exchange in the electoral market between political parties and

voters. Like in traditional marketing, each political party must offer a product that they intend to sell in the market. The party is attempting to market its product, which is the promise of good government. In some cases, the product may be a candidate's image, an ideology, or specific foreign policies. As a result, the entire marketing process is intended to market the product. For example, in the United States, the Democratic Party's primary product function was to sell the Obama Brand and change-based governance. In our case, we sold my friend, the mayor, as an agent to bring the people together and take them to the end of the journey.

2. **Distribution Function:** The distribution function refers to the conditions that govern the availability of an exchange offer to an exchange partner. The function is divided into two parts: campaign delivery and offering delivery. The campaign delivery function provides all relevant information about the political product to the primary exchange partner, the electorate. This includes disseminating information about crucial party policies and programmes, placing candidates in the appropriate channels, ensuring that the medium of distribution fits the party's ideology, and so on.

3. **Cost Function:** One of the primary functions of mainstream marketing is to sell a product that is less expensive than other products on the market, resulting in greater monetary satisfaction for the customer. The management of voters' attitudinal and behavioural barriers through calculated campaign strategies is referred to as the cost function in political marketing. The voter should receive all product information without having to pay for it.

4. **Communication Function:** Communication entails informing the primary exchange partner of the offer and its availability. It is frequently regarded as the heart of political marketing. For a political party, this entails providing political content, ideas, and information about future programmes and assisting in the interpretation and making sense of a complex political world. Often, the communication function entails simplifying political messages, taking a concise political stance, and so on. The communication function interacts with the distribution function's campaign delivery aspects—the latter provides the medium, while the former defines the content. The communication function specifies a dialogue with the exchange partners—a multidirectional flow of information and the establishment of a shared agenda.

5. **News Management Function:** This function is inextricably linked to the communication function. However, the news management function is aimed at secondary exchange partners or intermediaries, of which the media is a crucial component. In other words, it is the management of the candidate's and party's publicity. News management functions include public relations, media management, online advertising campaign management, etc. In the age of the communication revolution, news management is critical to the success of political marketing.

6. **Fundraising Function:** Fundraising is not an issue in mainstream marketing. Political marketing management, on the other hand, cannot exist without fundraising. In fact, the success of other functions is heavily reliant on the

fundraising function. A distinct fundraising function must be addressed in order to provide appropriate resources to the political actor. A political party's funding comes from various sources, including membership fees, donations, etc.

7. **Parallel Campaign Management Function:** This function describes the requirement of coordinating a political party's campaign management activities with those of parallel organisations. Coordination and synergistic use of managerial activities allow for more efficient campaign resource deployment. Furthermore, the use of parallel campaigns and endorsements from other organisations can increase the credibility of political messages.

8. **Internal Cohesion Management Function:** This function describes the need to coordinate a political party's campaign management activities with other organisations. Coordination and synergistic use of managerial activities allow for more effective campaign resource deployment. Additionally, the use of parallel campaigns and endorsements from other organisations can boost the credibility of political messages.

The Role and Impacts of Media in Political Communication

The media plays a strategic role in facilitating and developing new political communication techniques such as political advertising. This is because advertising is the most effective method of building and creating an image. Furthermore, the format allows political actors to deliver their messages directly to the public without the need for journalistic intervention.

Political advertisements are used in a variety of media, including television, radio, newspapers, billboards, and the cinema.

The media's contribution to politics and political communication, in general, is a constitutive feature of politics: democracy is founded on debate and politicians' communicative actions, and all citizens define and assign value to themselves, others, and the community. Furthermore, in an ideal democratic society, the media can play a variety of roles, including providing information, educating citizens, serving as a platform for public political discourse, providing publicity to the government as the society's watchdog, and serving as a channel for the advocacy of political viewpoints.

As the media evolves and plays an increasingly important role, one should never underestimate what it can do for oneself or one's adversary. Roses have thorns, and so does the media, which can cause national and anti-national strife and jeopardise social balance and harmony by presenting biased coverage, fuelling hatred and anarchy, and ignoring the concept of neutral journalism.

Moreover, technological advancements alter people's interactions, and "visibility" becomes more important for politicians. The more frequently prominent politicians appear on television, the more powerful they become. As a result of these changes, political institutions are forced to alter their political discourse, and new communication techniques emerge with "catch-all" politicians. The impact of political marketing on democracy would be determined by the public's willingness to participate in and respond to this type of political communication.

Obama Victory in 2008

With the advent of the world wide web, the history of modern political marketing underwent a significant shift. The Internet, and later social media, have played a significant role in defining the world's political leaders in the twenty-first century. Facebook, Twitter, and other digital tools greatly aided in the election of both former U.S. presidents Barack Obama and Donald Trump. In 2008, Obama's marketers, Jason Ralston and Ben Self, were the first to recognise and utilise the enormous potential of social media.

Although some may attribute Obama's victory solely to social media, the ability to mobilise digital activism to act as a channel for the propagation of the electoral message was at the heart of the digital strategy. In politics, social media is more than just a number of followers, fans, or posts; it also involves the ability to engage, which leads to effective electorate participation. The brilliant idea of Obama's political team was to bring digital militancy—which was already strong at the time—to the physical environment. The propagation of the face and name of the political aspirant is not only possible through the old marketing channels and tools (an active approach), but is boosted by the electorate, who truly believes—and, more importantly, funds—the "change" of the political reality (a passive phenomenon).

Political marketing has always evolved in tandem with the development of temporal human values such as civil freedom and democracy, shifting from a non-critical and sometimes misleading portrayal of the ruler (propaganda) who had gained power through arbitrary mechanisms to the notion that the aspirant ruler must first undergo thorough public scrutiny (this is where good political marketing comes into play) before being awarded political glory by a galvanised crowd. That is why the term "leader" best describes the main actor in the science of political marketing: he must be able to hypnotise the governed by instilling a genuine belief in CHANGE. If he wants to enlist more followers, he must be able to demonstrate his commitment to moral, ethical, and democratic values. Additionally, in this day and age, those followers are more aware and well-informed about the deceiving reality, even if hidden in a virtual, candid world. Political marketing is gradually establishing itself as a true science, with a set of practices, elements, and a culture on which modern politicians should rely and adhere, whether during an election campaign or to increase their political influence.

Trump and Cambridge Analytica

Remember how I mentioned this case at the beginning of this chapter? It's now time for me to go into more detail about what happened. What did Cambridge Analytica (CA) actually do? Cambridge Analytica and its parent company, SCL Group, went out of business in May 2018. However, Cambridge Analytica had been hired by Trump's successful 2016 presidential campaign, and the company is also rumoured to have played an important role in the Brexit Referendum Leave campaigns, although its role in the latter remains unclear. The company was inextricably linked to its parent company, SCL Group, and was frequently indistinguishable in practice. Both companies were involved in several other election campaigns around the world, including performing work in Indonesia, Nigeria, and Kenya, all of which received extensive media coverage in the aftermath of the Cambridge Analytica data scandal.

By way of background, SCL Group—based in the United Kingdom—joined U.S. far-right propagandist and former Breitbart editor Steve Bannon, U.S. right-wing billionaire and technologist Robert Mercer, and Mercer's daughter Rebekah Mercer in founding Cambridge Analytica. Alexander Nix, a British director at SCL, was the key figure in managing Cambridge Analytica data scientists and actively pursuing contracts. Although Cambridge Analytica was officially founded in 2015, its key players were already collaborating with several Republican candidates in the United States' 2014 midterm elections. Cambridge Analytica joined the Trump campaign in June 2016 after having previously worked on Ted Cruz's 2016 presidential primary campaign.

SCL Group had four divisions: SCL Defence (which ran defence contracts primarily with U.S. and U.K. state agencies), SCL Social (which ran development aid projects), SCL Elections (which ran the division most closely associated with Cambridge Analytica activities but which predated it by several years), and SCL Commercial (running contracts with the private sector, which Cambridge Analytica also did). While the two companies worked in a wide range of industries, the common thread was that they specialised in "public relations" campaigns aimed at behavioural change. This is a label well known to anthropologists of development. Think, for example, about condom use campaigns in HIV-affected countries.

Nigel Oakes founded the British think tank Behavioural Dynamics Institute (BDI) in 1990, and SCL's expertise grew from there. In 2010, the BDI described itself as an "academic institute that specialises in understanding influence and persuasion in order to change audiences' attitudes and behaviour." The institute "specialises in applying its methodology to military and political campaigns, where audiences are hostile or friendly, national or international." The BDI "methodology draws extensively from group and social psychology and incorporates semiotics, semantics, and many elements of cultural anthropology." The stated goals of the BDI hinted at ambitions that extended far beyond academic research. In practice, the distinction between the BDI and the SCL/Cambridge Analytica was blurred, with several personnel and projects straddling the academic and business operations.

Academic members and contributors named on their archived website came from various fields, including clinical and social psychology, sociology, political science, international relations, and media and communications. Many were based in academic social science departments in ostensibly "independent" units at prestigious universities, while others had overt ties to military and security agencies in the United Kingdom and the United States. Some had strong ties to both worlds. While academic interests listed included anthropology, none of those profiled with bios on the BDI website appear to have had graduate training in anthropology. There are, however, indications that anthropology may have played a more direct role, as journalist and disinformation expert Peter Pomerantsev claimed in his 2019 book on social media and propaganda:

Oakes pioneered surveys by teams of anthropology students, who, usually without revealing their mission, spent long periods penetrating a community, enquiring about who people hated and trusted, what they most desired, which friends would influence them, and what dictated how they behaved within a group.

Pomerantsev's account of SCL's pre-social media days appears to place a high value on the influence of long-term fieldwork on the development of SCL research techniques. And, of course, the countries where SCL worked in political—and later military and development campaigns—had long been the domain of anthropological knowledge, at least in Anglo-American academia.

Cambridge Analytica's more recent data-driven incarnation employed several data scientists and scientific knowledge from academia, specifically from the University of Cambridge. The name was chosen as an act of "prestige appropriation" and to indicate an active recruitment of Cambridge data scientists and the deployment of cutting-edge research on Internet psychographics developed at the university. According to leaked documents, Cambridge Analytica used the BDI methodology, which is centred on Target Audience Analysis (TAA), a method well established in Anglo-American military propaganda circles and has been discussed in numerous defence publications.

This method's alleged innovation in the field of propaganda and psychological operations (PSYOP) is that it aims to study individual, social, cultural, political, and economic characteristics of specific groups and their members prior to the launch of a specific campaign. This then informs the development of messages aimed at such groups or segments of them, which build on the knowledge gained about a variety of psychological and socio-cultural traits revealed by the analysis.

Messages are tailored to their intended audiences, and knowing such audiences is a critical component of successful behavioural change campaigns. The original TAA insights were expanded upon by Cambridge Analytica, which combined them with the power of big data, including, but not limited to, personality profiling of social media users with the goal of significantly increasing the effectiveness and reach of targeted messages.

The project's main goal was to reach approximately 9 million voters nationwide, with a "special emphasis" on New Hampshire, Pennsylvania, Virginia, North Carolina, Florida, Ohio, Iowa, Colorado, Nevada, and Michigan—those battleground states that could have gone either way (Republican or Democrat) in the election. The details on the target audience are sketchy, but the report suggests that most of the voters targeted by Cambridge Analytica digital media campaigns were Clinton voters who could be persuaded to vote for Trump instead of Clinton. However, it is suggested elsewhere in the same document that Republican voters were also targeted in "get out the vote" campaigns aimed at increasing their likelihood of voting. The most successful ads, according to the report, were run on Facebook and Google Search, but the full range of platforms utilized included YouTube, Twitter, Google Display Network, Snapchat, Pandora Internet Radio, email, and traditional television.

****

Companies today use analytics, consumer perception, and marketing strategies to move a candidate from point A to point B. Politicians must employ a variety of strategies to appeal to all demographics. To increase voter conversion and retention, it is critical to integrate digital and traditional political marketing forms. Traditional touchpoints such as direct mail, telemarketing, and canvassing are still essential tools for reaching specific demographics, particularly the senior population, which has a high voter turnout rate. E-mail marketing and social media channels are becoming increasingly important. E-mails are primarily used to generate funds to cover expenses. On the other hand, politicians must be careful not to overuse marketing to the point of annoying potential donors.

Social media is an important tool for reaching out to younger audiences. Campaigns also use the analytical capabilities of social media platforms to better understand how voters interact with the candidates. Finally, perhaps the most important tool in political marketing strategy is the importance of media and public relations in politics. Having your candidate in the news on a regular basis raises their brand recognition among voters. Candidates strive to balance media exposure in such a way that they appear relatable to voters (Saturday Night Live appearances, for example) while also maintaining their professionalism. Given the constant scrutiny of today's political world and its leaders, politicians must successfully "brand" themselves if they hope to win the votes of the American people—and the position for which they aspire.

The Impacts of Political Marketing through Social Media
Web 2.0, a term used to describe existing interactive web applications that allow for the creation and exchange of User Generated Content (UGC), is responsible for the development of social media. Web 2.0 combines numerous features, making it a one-stop-shop for distributing multimedia content

and blogging. Blogs, web forums, instant chats, and social networking sites such as Facebook, YouTube, and Twitter are examples of well-known social media platforms. These platforms enable users to create online relationships or communities where people who share a common trust in a political leader can develop loyalty to that leader and party.

When a voter trusts and is loyal to a particular party, the voter will have a strong inclination to vote for that political party. Empirical evidence has established that when voters have a strong level of confidence in a political party and candidate, they will vote for them. Conversely, when this trust does not exist, the voters either vote for the opposition or simply do not vote. For this reason, the study seeks to investigate whether social media usage influences trust, loyalty, and ultimately voting intention. It is envisaged that the study will formulate interests that can interact, engage, and share opinions and knowledge. As social media content is user-generated, it lends itself to being perceived as personal, genuine, and transparent.

In the political arena, social media has offered users new channels for distributing and consuming political information. Instead of receiving political information from other media such as TV, print, radio, and other formats, users now receive political communication from familiar sources via postings of friends and acquaintances. Because of this accessibility, politics has become part of the daily lives of young people, which further enhances their interest in the subject. Gillmor (2006) affirms this assertion and adds that since social media consists mainly of user-generated content, users can discover views that are not well represented in traditional news outlets, enhancing their curiosity and interest in seeking more information online.

Social media provides political parties with the advantage of addressing voters rapidly and directly. Politicians can easily publish their opinions on personal websites, weblogs, micro-blogging sites, and social networking platforms, thus mobilising voters and circumventing the selection criteria of journalists.

Political marketing has an impact on the health of democracy. Some academics believe that it benefits the democratic system. For starters, political marketing expands the number of information sources as well as the amount of information available to voters. Second, it aids in the development of relationships between candidates and constituents. This is due to the fact that political marketing employs an exchange model between politicians and the general public, similar to producers and consumers. Third, because the practice of this political communication technique is clearly voter-oriented, the public has a plethora of options and information from which to choose.

Despite these positive effects, political marketing has some drawbacks. Initially, political marketing campaigns are commercialised, reducing political values and substantives. Second, as the role of the media and consultants grows in importance, it will eventually replace the role of the parties. Third, an obvious effect of political marketing is the use of money politics. This is because high levels of competition and democracy imply a free market. Fourth, political marketing, which typically uses advertising as a medium to promote the candidate, tends to manipulate the public and is thus harmful to democracy.

The Political Brand

Political branding, which we have briefly touched on above, refers to how the general public perceives a political organisation or individual. It is more comprehensive than the product; whereas a product has distinct functional components, such as a politician and policy, a brand is intangible and psychological. A political brand is the public's overarching feeling, impression, association, or image of a politician, political organisation, or nation. Political branding assists the party or candidate in changing or maintaining reputation and support, creating a sense of identity with the party or its candidates, and establishing a trusting relationship between political elites and consumers. It assists political consumers in quickly understanding what a party or candidate stands for and distinguishing a candidate or party from the competition.

When a country, state, town, or district is in the midst of an election, the buzz begins to build. Given the high level of interest in consuming news and opinions on this subject, getting the marketing and branding aspects right is critical. As we watch (and many of us participate in) the electioneering and campaigning processes taking place in various states across the country, there is an interesting drama unfolding in terms of image projection.

After all, elections are the new form of entertainment in many ways. Unlike in the past, when it was a political purist's pursuit, today, everyone is involved and participative. What do the elections lack? They have it all—protagonists and antagonists, incumbents and anti-incumbents, triumph and defeat, mystery, suspense, heroics, and expected and unanticipated outcomes.

It's an exciting, thrilling roller coaster ride right in front of you. It's the best spectator sport there is. Why would the reader or viewer not be interested?

Building a powerful political brand is a considerable challenge that can take years—and an undertaking that can be destroyed in a single blow. And because this is not the usual world of fast-moving consumer goods (FMCG), consumer durables, services, and so on, there are many challenges in contouring the brand values and core brand messages. Let me enumerate the differences with examples to clarify the points expressed above: Each voter is equally important. There is no distinction between rich and poor, urban and rural, men and women, old and young. Every vote carries the same weight. In traditional brand marketing, the 80:20 rule kicks in, where you focus on heavy users who make up 20% of your consumer base but provide you with an 80% return on investment. However, in the political world, every vote counts.

Surprisingly, the urban consumer votes in lower numbers than the rural counterpart. This is supported by research and data. There is only one action day per campaign, and that day is election day. In contrast to regular brands, where you can build up advertising and hope that the consumer takes additional action to understand, check out, and—ideally—buy the product, an election only lasts one day. If the consumer does not "buy" you that day, the story is over. The importance of a slogan cannot be overstated. The hook is what will help you connect with your audience like nothing else. It encapsulates the culmination of your strategy in a few succinct words that should ring true. Your slogan should be liked and used by people in everyday conversation.

Think about Barack Obama's infectious and optimistic campaign slogan, "Yes we can!" in 2008. These three simple words embodied—in political terms—challenge, possibility, ability, permission, and opportunity. Or, thinking back a bit farther, you may recall perhaps the most memorable of them all: Saatchi and Saatchi's 1978 campaign "Labour Isn't Working" for Margaret Thatcher. Or, closer to home for those in India, Lal Bahadur Shastri's "Jai Jawan Jai Kisan" or Atal Bihari Vajpayee's "Ab ki bari Atal Bihari"—both of which saluted soldiers and farmers. The 2004 general elections in India were perhaps the best example of two powerful slogans combined. Whereas the BJP's slogan was "India Shining," the Congress' slogan was "Aam aadmi ko kya mila." A strong emotional connection is something that all of these have in common. National esteem, individual safety, and a compatible ideology.

Every medium is significant. It's critical to appear on television to effectively sell fast-moving goods like soaps and shampoos to remind consumers of your brand. High-ticket or high-tech items necessitate rational mediums, and thus are best served by print media. Radio, outdoor, and below-the-line collaterals are commonly referred to as secondary or support media. Not in the world of politics, though. If you want to reach out to the rural consumer who works in the field or rides his bike to work, his primary media will be radio, wall paintings, stickers, banners, and posters. Rural women who work in the agrarian economy or their own kitchens are also included in this group.

The game has changed as a result of social media. When you look at social media handles, you will notice that some political leaders have the most followers. People tend to want to know what they are saying or believing if they are inspirational and popular. It's worth noting that while the BJP has 17.6 million Twitter followers, Prime Minister Narendra Modi has 75.4 million. Congress has 8.4 million followers on Twitter to Rahul Gandhi's 19.6 million followers. As a result, in the political game, individuals can outnumber corporations. While Facebook and Twitter are the social media platforms of choice for their generalist profiles, an increasing number of politicians are also moving to Instagram. This would assist them in reaching millennials.

What about the Millennials and Gen Z? TikTok and Snapchat are said to have made their way into political media during the most recent U.S. elections. YouTube is the world's second most popular social media platform, and it is currently being used for the UP elections. Engaging the public via a live video based on the 9 p.m. prime time TV schedule is outdated. Instead, politicians can now break their own news and engage in real-time conversations with their constituents. For example, in the United States, many politicians regularly live stream on Facebook and Instagram to interact with voters and non-voters alike. Instead of simply talking at voters, live video encourages meaningful and personable conversations. This is more common in the Western world, but it is likely to make a big impact in India as well. With almost imperceptible lead times, political parties must maintain contact with their constituents. Unlike the usual rule of engaging on social media twice or three times per week, it is recommended to post and comment on a daily basis in the political arena. Sometimes you don't have a choice. There are counterarguments. There are new concepts. And you must continue to produce material until it reaches the customer—the voter.

Mobile is the primary medium for reaching a large population, particularly young people. Around 52% of the world's population is under thirty. Coupled with the fact that, according to Statista, the current global smartphone user population is 6.648 billion, it means that 83.72 percent of the world's population owns a smartphone. This is the most important tool to consider in current and future elections. The majority of young people get their news from online editions, news shorts, Twitter, and other social media platforms. They want opinions and views more than straight news. It is critical to create for a smaller screen. Posters, memes, music videos, and stickers are what go viral and generate a lot of buzz. More than anything else, the strategy must be properly crafted.

This isn't a region or a sub-section. You're dealing with the entire country. Or, in the case of assembly elections, the whole state. Some of our states are larger than many European countries combined. First and foremost, a party must determine its election strategy. What will be the strategy? Ideally, you want to target every consumer. So, what language will you communicate with them in? English or vernacular as the national language? This will eventually lead to the Brand Proposition. Every political brand should be founded on a strong, distinct consumer proposition. Brands must have points of parity in their propositions in order to compete (for example, every political brand represents the Indian voter) as well as compelling points of difference, such as a party that talks to the youth, or a party that is secular, or a party that drives growth.

Political brands typically promise economic development, attractive domestic and foreign investments, rapid and massive job creation, and poverty alleviation. These are the kinds of promises that every political party makes as elections approach. They are universal needs of the majority of voters, and a political brand that does not provide them does not stand a chance. As a result, the point of differentiation must come from a completely different dimension. This could be a commitment to growth, to better meet the needs of a specific region or group, or to illustrate a track record of superior performance.

Every party would like to target the entire voter base, which would necessitate segmentation. Is that possible, though? That means spending an indefinite amount of money to get voters to see your messages until they register. In terms of media costs, this would be prohibitively expensive. Typically, a target segmentation exercise is required. Who are you speaking with? Who is more likely to listen to you? Regular brands will occasionally use a celebrity or a spokesperson to endorse a product to give it a boost. Regular brands can get away without doing it, but it is an absolute necessity in a political scenario. Because these individuals represent ideologies that the consumer believes in, it is a very effective tool.

The Republicans were represented in the 2021 U.S. elections by incumbent President Donald Trump. The Democrats needed to field the best candidate possible to counter his popularity. There were no announcements for a long time. The party appeared to be adrift. The political brand wars began when Joe Biden became the chosen face. As I mentioned at the outset, when brands are at odds, the consumer has the most fun. They keep a close eye on the issues, repartee, and salvos. All eyes are on the leadership, and it is critical at every level for the leader to connect across age groups—but especially the youth. Some countries are in the midst of state elections, and the excitement is palpable. Given the high level of interest in consuming news and opinions on this subject, it's critical to nail the marketing and branding aspects.

Three Steps to Creating a Strong Political Brand

If you want to see electoral success in this day and age, you must first establish a strong political brand for yourself. If you don't have a presence on the Internet, you might as well not be running at all. Not just any online brand, but a solid, well-thought-out political brand is what you need to achieve success. By following these steps, you can become more organised and improve the clarity of your political statements. These three simple steps will help build a robust political brand from scratch and elevate your name from the depths of obscurity to the forefront of public consciousness.

Step 1: Identify and Define Your Political Branding

When defining your political brand, it is critical to communicate your message concisely. To be effective in your pitch, you must explain how you are uniquely positioned to serve your target audience. The target audience is critical. Please keep in mind that if you're talking to everyone, you're really talking to no one.

Additionally, genuineness is essential for building a powerful political brand in today's world. If people do not believe that they can relate to you on a personal level, they will not vote for you in the election.

Remember that when developing a digital brand for your political campaign, it is critical to keep in mind that the brand must tell a story about the campaign. To persuade your target audience that your principles are sound, you should aim to tell a story.

While there are numerous effective ways to craft a compelling story, you should tell your story in such a way that voters believe you understand their concerns and are capable of resolving their issues. Incorporating your personal experiences into your solutions is an excellent way to accomplish this.

Create Your Elevator Pitch

You will be able to define your political brand better if you create an elevator pitch. This short soundbite enables your target audience to grasp the essence of who you are and what you have to offer in a matter of seconds. In addition to social media, your elevator pitch will be referenced in articles and other online publications as well as on your website.

It will be much easier to navigate the process of digital branding if you first understand what you want from your political brand.

Keep these important considerations in mind when developing your political brand's elevator pitch:

- It shouldn't sound too scripted. Rather than creating a strict script, remember a few key points and tailor them to suit different situations.

- If you want your elevator pitch to be effective, it can't sound like a pitch at all. Just quickly and honestly describe what you do.

- Your pitch should be tailored to your audience. Your political pitch should be flexible. You will address fellow candidates, your local association, the press, and the public differently.

- Keep it short and simple. Your pitch should not be longer than thirty seconds.

Create Your Slogan

Your slogan needs to do more than just say that you're running for office. You will need to consider the motivational traits of your leadership. Also, factor in the opportunities your administration will provide voters.

When you create your political slogan, you want to be seen as unique. It is just a few words that people will associate with you, and that will define your political brand.

A few slogans come to mind immediately when you think of political candidates. Slogans like: "Yes we can," "Patriotism, protection, and prosperity," "Peace and prosperity," and "Putting people first," are clear descriptions of what these political candidates were hoping to accomplish while in office.

Step 2: Build Your Political Brand

Before getting involved with a politician's campaign in real life, people almost always look them up online. In most cases, your target audience will interact with your digital brand, then decide if they want to support you or not based on their experience.

As a result, your digital brand is key when spreading the word about your entire political campaign. Without a solid online political brand, it won't matter how many town hall meetings you go to, how many hands you shake, or whether or not you kiss babies.

If you ignore the digital arena, people will be able to talk about you however they like online unrestrained. As a result of your absence, you will be powerless to protect your reputation and brand online.

Build Your Home Base

To ensure that your audience receives the correct information the first time, you must focus on building your home base. For most of us, our home base is our website or blog.

Your home base is a critical component of your digital brand. It is the first place many people will go to learn more about you, and it can either make or break their first impression of you as a politician. Your home base must be factual, but it must also be engaging, user-friendly, and look professional.

When creating your home base, keep these four things in mind:

1. Domain Name

This is your digital address. People will use it to find your website. Some popular domain name providers are GoDaddy and NameCheap.

2. Website Building Software

This is the software you can use to build your site. Some of the more popular web builders you might have heard of are WordPress, Wix, Squarespace, and Weebly.

3. Web Host

This is the storage unit where your website content lives online.

4. Website Template Design

A website template is a pre-made website design. It allows you to create a professional-looking website without hiring a website designer. If you are using a self-hosted website builder like WordPress, you can find great templates at WooThemes and Mojo Marketplace.

Build Your Email List

If you want to succeed in political branding, get serious about building your email list. Your email list is one of the most valuable assets for your brand because it allows you to initiate contact with your audience.

Instead of waiting at your home base, hoping they'll drop by the party, you're virtually knocking on their door with a personal invitation.

Adding an opt-in form on your website is also a great way to get your target audience's attention and encourage them to sign up for your email list. You can include these on the side of your website, at the bottom, or as a scrolling pop-up. It all depends on your target audience.

Build Your Social Media Accounts

Your primary objective for building your social media accounts is to focus on how to be social, not on how to do social.

Being relatable to your target audience will separate you from the competition. Talk to people on social media the same way you would engage in real life. After all, just because you are communicating with people online doesn't mean that you aren't communicating with people.

Talk The Talk

When first starting on social media, it is best to focus only on one site. Having too many accounts can be overwhelming. Also, if you are spread too thin, it will be difficult to build a truly authentic and effective presence.

Placing yourself in the conversations of constituents is one way to increase your visibility. You should look for opportunities to engage with the community, as reaching out to the people you represent makes them feel seen and heard by you. This can be the difference between getting or losing someone's vote.

Step 3: Manage Your Political Brand

This component of your political brand will be a continuous presence in your day-to-day activities. It may be in your best interests to seek a digital branding service to manage and build on this work on your behalf from time to time.

Guest Blogging

One great way to increase your online visibility is through guest blogging. If your content is posted on a site with a larger or different audience from your own, guest blogging will allow you to expand your digital presence.

When picking a place to guest blog, it is essential to remember your values and choose a site that shares similar values. You'll also want to check the blogger's guidelines to see if they accept guest posts. If everything lines up, you can contact them and share why you'd be an excellent fit for their blog.

When going through the process of finding the right blog to guest post on, make a list of five blogs that you'd be willing to work with and reach out to them. The odds are pretty good that at least one will be interested in your contributions. Also, if your pitch is well thought out, you might just get a chance to write for all of them.

Repurpose Your Content

When creating an effective digital brand, it can feel like the key to success is endlessly pumping out content. However, few people have the time to create new content all day, every day. Fortunately, there is an easier way.

Trying to create an eBook every month or coming up with new topics for blog posts is simpler when you re-use pre-existing content.

Here are some helpful examples:
You can take your most popular blog post about a particular topic and turn it into an eBook. Then you can repurpose the eBook as a SlideShare presentation. Or you can take that same eBook and turn it into a month's worth of blog posts. Or you can turn that blog post into an infographic or video. There are endless possibilities!

Plus, everyone likes to consume content in different ways. Some may want to read an eBook or whitepaper, while another is fond of video or audio content. Repurposing your content will allow users to consume content in the ways that they like best.

Practice Batching Content

Batching is the process of doing a lot of similar things at the same time. For instance, you wouldn't make a single cookie at a time. You'd make a whole batch of them, right? Well, the same is true for writing.

Half the challenge is just getting into that creative writing space where we can produce.

You're going to save a lot of time by knocking out multiple posts at once.

Final Thoughts

Your political brand is who you are to most people. Remember that most people will never see you in person, which means that they will only have your brand to guide them in their decision-making process.

This is why following these three steps will be crucial for your political campaign. You need to define your brand, build your brand, and monitor your brand to achieve maximum success in the digital world. It will give you the political boost you need and make you a household name.

A Political Campaign

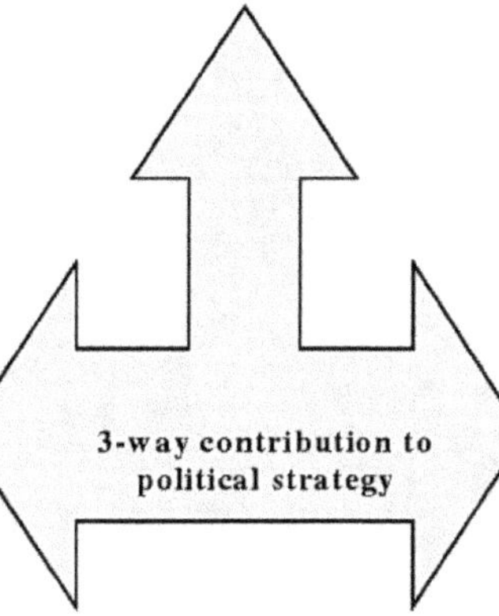

Election Campaign

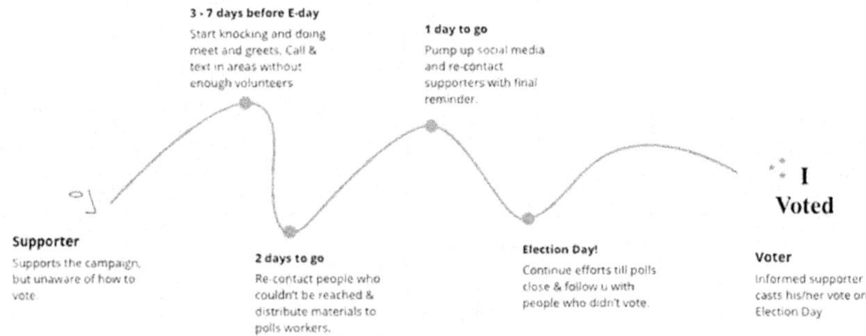

Chapter Four

The Campaign: People, Strategies, Processes, and Tactics

What is the Campaign All About in Politics?

A political campaign is a well-organised effort to influence decision-making within a specific group. The term 'political campaign' is frequently used in democracies to refer to electoral campaigns where representatives are elected, or referendums are decided. In modern times, the most high-profile political campaigns are centred on general elections and candidates for head of state or head of government, often a president or prime minister. Election campaigns are held to allow for a free and open debate about who is a better representative and, as a result, which party will form a better government.

I know that definition sounds a little bookish, but as we progress and you see more content, you'll fully understand what I'm aiming for and why it's critical we start this way.

The road to becoming a mayor, governor, president, or prime minister is lengthy, costly, and exhausting. Becoming a candidate is only the first step in the electoral process.

Successful candidates must persuade voters that they deserve their individual votes as well as, in some cases, garner the critical votes of electors (like America, where they have the Electoral College).

A political campaign is all about persuading voters. Advertising, theme songs, stump speeches, and even negative campaigning have existed since the beginning of the organised system of governance, and each technological advancement has provided new opportunities for candidates to persuade voters. Campaign advertising that attacks an opponent's personality, record, or opinion is the most common form of negative campaigning. There are two types of ads in negative campaigning: attack and contrast. The negative aspects of the opponent are the sole focus of attack advertisements. Negative advertisements tend to focus on candidates' personal characteristics, whereas positive advertisements focus on significant policy differences.

The modern democratic era, however, has brought about significant changes in the political world, particularly concerning political communication practices. In election campaigns, there has been a considerable shift in how politicians manage and design political campaign strategies in order to gain public support. As a result, in a modern, open, and transparent political competition, contestants require a method for distributing political products to the public, such as new ideas, issues, party ideology, programmes, and leadership characteristics. To win the election, they must be able to implement new political communication strategies that are more oriented toward voters and understand how this can be done by implementing marketing strategies to promote the candidate and their political values. Science and marketing approaches are useful in this context for political institutions.

As a result, many political actors, including the government, parties, politicians, and interest groups, adopted and widely used political marketing in their political campaigning. According to some academics, it is an obvious manifestation of a "contemporary political communication" phenomenon.

Political leaders should be able to define the characteristics of their political brand these days. To succeed in the political arena, they must understand, identify, and employ the most appropriate communication mechanism. This enables them to create an accurate perception of their political image in the market that is strictly linked to the characteristics of their brand to achieve the above goals. For these reasons, it is essential to have measurement methods and results that can be compared over time.

The media has evolved dramatically, and today's campaign strategies incorporate statistical analysis and the science of influence and affect. Today, every word, every action, and even a candidate's perceived thoughts are paraded in front of the public. Many of the methods for persuading voters, however, remain essentially the same.

In this chapter, I will explore some of the key players in this process, including: Who were the campaign spin doctors, the campaign advisers, the ad agencies, and the PR agencies who ran the most extensive campaigns? What tricks did these players use to convince the people to vote in their favour?

The Campaign Spin Doctors

Depending on our point of view, the term "spin" can mean a variety of things, including both negative and positive ideals. We can define a spin doctor as the person or group of people (such as a political aide) who ensures that others interpret an event from a particular point of view. In another moment, within seconds, we may say that "spin doctors," "spinmeisters," or "spinmeisteresses" refer to those who work in the fields of public relations, polling, or media consulting and who develop deceptive or misleading messages. Whichever way we define the terms, we know that this group of persons, the political "spin doctors," are always hard at work behind the scenes—no matter how many times an election season comes around. They are the campaign advisers, social media strategists, press secretaries, and others who craft political messages to assist their candidates in "selling" themselves. They are the strong individuals you must have by your side before, during, and, in many cases, after the election process.

"Spin doctors" have the option of commanding media attention or maintaining anonymity. Jamie Shea, who served as NATO's Press Secretary throughout the Kosovo War, Charlie Whelan, and Alastair Campbell are just a few of the most notable figures from the United Kingdom.

Gordon Campbell, a former journalist who rose to the position of Tony Blair's Press Secretary, served as the driving force behind an administration that effectively communicated its message to the public through the news media. He played an important role in key decisions, with advisors referring to him as a 'Deputy Prime Minister' who was inextricably linked to Blair. Campbell cites how he persuaded Rupert Murdoch, during a meeting in July 1995, to positively report an upcoming Blair speech, garnering support from the Sun and the Times, two popular British newspapers, to write stories about Blair in a positive light. Campbell also mentions how he persuaded Rupert Murdoch, during a meeting in July 1995, to positively report an incoming Blair speech, garnering support from the Sun and the Times. Afterward, Campbell acknowledged that his and the government's spinning had contributed to the electorate's growing distrust of politicians, and he asserted that the practise of spinning had to be discontinued.

Campbell's work was praised and respected by "spin doctors" such as Shea and others. Shea's media strategy was utterly non-existent in 1999, at the start of NATO's intervention in Kosovo, before the arrival of Campbell and his team. Shea learned from Campbell how to organise his team to deliver what he desired to be in the media, which resulted in Shea being recognised for his efforts by former President Bill Clinton.

Take, for another peculiar example, Kellyanne Conway, who served as Donald Trump's campaign manager during the 2016 United States presidential campaign. Her silver tongue made frequent appearances on news programmes to spin something controversial Trump had said, often sweeping outrageous claims made by the candidate under the rug and ultimately persuading Americans to vote for him. Several of the tactics that Ms. Conway used to muddy the message repeatedly are covered in this chapter.

Spin doctors are also a source of concern in the United Kingdom. Andreas Whittam Smith, the founding editor of the Independent newspaper, has claimed that the business of Westminster has largely transformed into a brand, blaming this on the nature of the political establishment. His book describes how young people interested in politics used to jump right out of university into positions as political advisers, policy analysts in policy research organisations, and lobbyists for organisations representing special interests, all of which coincided with the Parliamentary session.

As a result, it was not surprising to see statistics in a Who Governs Britain? report from 2015, revealing that approximately 60% of Labour Members of Parliament were 'fully paid-up members of the political class.' We can tell that democracy has been compromised by looking at statistics like this one.

These individuals join political parties with far too much insider knowledge to be able to take an unbiased and unbranded approach to their political campaigns. Throughout the shaky Brexit campaign, we saw evidence of this. They have all been involved in politics since they were students at university, including David Cameron and Boris Johnson, as well as their Chief Lieutenants George Osborne and Michael Gove.

Spin doctors went berserk in the lead-up to the Australian federal election. Earlier, Georgina Downer, the Liberal candidate for the Adelaide seat of Mayo, released an anti-ALP campaign video that featured Jim, a retired South Coaster of 72 years, as the main character.

I and others played our roles for the mayor in our small Alpine town of Kitzbühel in western Austria, as well as in other places. When it comes to election projects, you simply cannot do without capable hands. Political spin doctors are simply a practical necessity in today's world, given how the media controls and influences the flow of information. Politicians must overcome media bias and prejudice with the assistance of spin doctors to communicate their message effectively.

As a result of the introduction of social media, the general public now has greater access to news, making it more difficult for politicians to stand out. As political parties seek to distinguish themselves from one another, they are increasingly employing political marketing strategies to achieve this objective. Spin doctors are an important component, and these marketing strategies are becoming increasingly important to political parties when it comes to winning elections.

Of course, the very definition of the term "spin" is debatable, and it, along with the phrase "fake news," has emerged as a convenient retort for those who reject any version of events that does not reflect their own point of view, regardless of how legitimate the claim is. On the other hand, what happened in 2018 with Trump and Cambridge Analytica has made the general public more aware and fearful of what spin doctors are capable of accomplishing for their clients or candidates.

Forms of Spin
"Spin" is achieved by providing a deliberately biased interpretation of an event or campaign in an effort to influence public opinion about a particular organisation or public figure, such as a politician. However, while traditional public relations and advertising can manage the presentation of facts, the

term "spin" is frequently used to refer to the use of deceptive, manipulative, and disingenuous tactics to achieve the desired outcome.

Because of the frequent association between spin and press conferences, it is common to refer to the room in which press conferences (particularly government press conferences) take place as a "spin room."

The reframing or modification of public perception of a particular issue or event is one of the most common strategies employed in "spinning," and it is used to mitigate any negative impact on public opinion that the issue or event may have on the public. A company whose best-selling product turns out to have a significant safety problem may choose to "reframe" the issue by criticising the safety of its main competitor's products or by emphasising the dangers associated with the entire product category in to avoid a public relations disaster. The use of a "catchy" slogan or sound bite that can assist in persuading the general public of the company's biased point of view, among other methods, can accomplish this. By employing this strategy, the company may be able to divert the public's attention away from the negative aspects of its product, which will be beneficial to the company.

Paid media advisors and media consultants are most often hired as contractors to provide spinning services to clients. Companies with large numbers of in-house employees and sophisticated units with expertise in spinning issues are common among the largest and most powerful organisations. When it comes to manipulating or deceiving the public, some politicians and political staff have been accused of employing deceptive "spin" tactics in the 1990s and 2000s. This is the case even though spin is generally considered a private-sector strategy. When someone uses spin, they may do things like: releasing potentially damaging information at the end of their workday on the last day before a long weekend; cherry-picking quotes from previous speeches made by their employer or an opposing politician to give the impression that they advocate a particular position; and purposefully spreading false information about an opposing politician or candidate that casts them in a negative light, among other things.

Spin Techniques

Some spin techniques include:

- Selectively presenting facts and quotes that support one's position is known as "cherry-picking." For example, a pharmaceutical company could choose only two trials where their product shows a positive effect and ignore hundreds of unsuccessful trials, or a politician's staff could handpick short speech quotations from past years which appear to show their candidate's support for a certain position.

- Non-denial denial – A statement that seems or is intended to act as a direct denial to an allegation, but which, when taken literally or examined closely, does not deny the allegation at all. The phrase is most commonly associated with evasive answers of politicians facing scrutiny or accusations of misconduct.

- Non-apology apology – A statement in the form of an apology that does not express remorse, or assigns fault to those ostensibly receiving the apology.

- "Mistakes were made" is an example of distancing language, commonly used as a rhetorical device, whereby a speaker acknowledges that a situation was managed inappropriately but evades any direct responsibility. The expression focuses on the action, omitting any actor, via the passive voice, and "mistakes" are framed in an indirect sense that does not imply intent. A less evasive active voice construction would focus on the actor, such as: "I made mistakes" or "John Doe made mistakes."

- Speaking in a way that assumes unproven claims or avoids the question

- "Burying bad news" involves announcing unpopular things when the media is expected to be focusing on other news. In some cases, governments have released potentially controversial reports on summer long weekends. Sometimes "other news" is deliberately supplied.

- Misdirection and diversion occur when a government leaks a story to the news to limit the coverage of a more damaging story circulating. New Labour used this tactic to reduce the coverage of Foreign Secretary Robin Cook's affair. This was achieved by leaking a story that a previous Governor of Hong Kong was under investigation by MI6.

- Limited hangout - Propaganda in which a selected portion of a scandal, criminal act, sensitive or classified information, etc. is revealed or leaked, without telling the whole story.

- Rewarding like-minded or amenable journalists with stories. During the Rhodesia crisis of 1964, Harold Wilson formulated a list of journalists that he trusted to write stories that aligned with the government's opinion.

- Preventing access to journalists or broadcasters that are reporting in ways the spin doctor disapproves of. An example is the World at One being ignored by New Labour in the build up to the 1997 general election due to an interview they held with Blair that asked difficult questions, leading to interviews being handed to other stations.

- For years, businesses have used fake or misleading customer testimonials by editing/spinning customers to reflect a much more satisfied experience than was actually the case. In 2009, the Federal Trade Commission updated its laws to include measures to prohibit this type of "spinning" and has been enforcing these laws as of late.

Campaign Tactics and Techniques

The term "tactics" is commonly used to designate the ways resources are deployed and directed within a broader strategy to reach the desired outcomes. Tactics are the social action activities that you use to achieve your goals and objectives, whereas the strategy is the sequencing of these in a logical and strategic way.

Different techniques may contribute to a single tactic or theory of change. However, the terms "tactics" and "techniques" are often used interchangeably. Common campaigning techniques include the following:

- Campaign advertising (e.g., using posters, radio and TV announcements)
- Attracting media attention (e.g., with press conferences and stunts)
- Demonstrations, rallies, marches, and other forms of mass meetings
- Using traditional arts to raise awareness or initiate community dialogue
- Electronic action-alerts via the Internet and mobile phones
- Using new media channels to spread messages (e.g., social networks, videos, blogs, Twitter, etc.)
- Mobilising volunteer campaign activists to influence peer groups (e.g., by organising community events or private house parties)
- Distribution of campaign merchandise, such as caps, bags, and wristbands
- Organisation of or participation in specialised conferences
- Lobbying key decision-makers

Since campaigning is a multi-faceted set of activities, the number of techniques that can be used is virtually unlimited.

Overt and Covert Spin Tactics

British researcher Ivor Gaber talked about "overt" and "covert" tactics used by press secretaries in the Blair government in the U.K.

Overt refers to standard or benign public relations tactics, such as writing press releases, staging events, giving speeches, and appearing in the media.

On the other hand, covert refers to a range of cynical techniques to manage information. These are the more malign tactics most people associate with "spin."

The list below contains a wide range of "covert" tactics drawn from research and personal experience. Each of these tactics is employed in a bid to exert control over the way the news media reports the message:

- **The Leak:** these are strategic leaks politicians or their staff offer to journalists in exchange for no scrutiny. In other words, you only get the leak if you promise not to seek comments from the opposing side or other critics. This is increasing and is a real problem.

- **The Freeze:** "freezing" or punishing journalists for negative reporting.

- **The Spray:** a form of bullying and intimidation, spraying is another way of punishing journalists for negative coverage. Many political reporters who file an unfavourable story can expect to "cop a spray" over the phone after it's published.

- **The Drip:** the act of keeping favoured reporters on a drip of exclusive information.

- **Staying on Message**: the goal of every public appearance or interview by a politician. In itself, it's not a malign tactic, but the constant repetition of the same messages without answering questions can be a form of obfuscation.

- **Pivoting** refers to politicians shifting away from a difficult question or issue to the one they want to talk about.

- **The Vomit Principle:** this rule of thumb is widely referred to in political offices. The idea is that if you repeat something so often you feel like vomiting, only then is it likely to be cutting through with the public.

- **Playing a Dead Bat**: this refers to not responding to a media inquiry or giving a minimal response in an effort to kill the story.

- **The truth, but Not the Whole Truth:** this refers to being selective with what one reveals, sharing only the most beneficial or least damaging information.

- **Throwing Out the Bodies/Taking Out the Garbage:** these tactics are used to disclose damaging information under cover of a major distraction. The classic example often used is that of Jo Moore, a media adviser in the Blair government in the U.K. On the day of the 9/11 attacks, she sent out an email saying: "It is now a very good day to get out anything we want to bury. Councillors' expenses?" Other common days to bury bad news are Christmas Eve, New Year's Eve, Grand Final Day, Melbourne Cup Day, or during a distraction like a royal visit.

- **Get Rid of It Now:** this tactic aims to release all of the damaging information on an issue at one time, so the negative story can be dealt with quickly rather than allowing it to bleed on for weeks in the media. One media adviser I interviewed explained it like this: "It's a truism in politics. If you've got to eat a shit sandwich, you've got to eat it straight away… The advice was always, 'Get rid of it now. Go and deal with it now.'"

- **Fire-Breaking:** setting up or staging a diversion to distract attention away from another issue. In the film Wag the Dog, the U.S. president fabricates a war in Albania to distract from a sex scandal. Less extreme examples would be launching a new policy to distract from a negative issue in an attempt to shift the media's attention.

- **Kite-Flying:** this means testing or floating an idea before making a commitment to announce it.

- **Feeding or Starving a Story:** feeding a story means keeping it alive by commenting on it in the media. Starving a story means starving it of oxygen by not commenting on it. The theory is that the media will get bored and move on after a while.

- **Keeping Out of the Media/Being a Small Target:** this is a useful tactic if the politician is unpopular and it affects the polls, has a controversial portfolio, or is an accident-prone poor performer.

- **Flying Under the Radar** refers to just quietly getting on with things without publicising them.

- **Dishing Dirt:** this is where old claims suddenly emerge publicly before or during an election in an effort to smear someone's reputation. The "dirt" can come from outside or inside a party. It's a tactic used to try to destroy someone's political career.

- **Dog-Whistling:** using specific subtle language and messages to target a particular section of the audience.

- **Wedging:** this tactic involves raising an issue that is popular in the electorate and sensitive to the party you are opposing in an effort to "wedge" them into a difficult position and sow division within the party.

Campaign Strategies and Processes

There is no 'correct' way to organise a campaign, and there is no one 'right' answer. Every election campaign can be compared to a football game. We know that the football field has rules that have governed it for centuries, and while each match is different, the same rulebook governs each game. The movement of the player on the field and the direction of the ball, on the other hand, are never predictable. Instead, these are guided by intuition and the demand of the time at any given moment. However, campaign organisation is not dissimilar from the previous concept in that you use your knowledge and experience to determine how the resources you have available can be used to fit the situation and achieve the desired result. In fact, in all our mayoral contests, we never used the same playbook more than once for this very reason.

There are always new and different things that we can do, but just because you are trying out new activities or methods in a campaign does not mean that you are following a strategic approach to it. Strategy entails conducting a thorough analysis of your situation and deciding on the actions that will have the greatest impact. These strategic actions may be 'old' or 'new,' but they will be tailored for maximum effect.

A more adaptive definition of campaign is an organised, purposeful effort to bring about change that should be guided by careful planning and consideration.

Within the overarching campaign strategy, several processes run parallel to one another, each requiring its own sub-strategy, complete with formative research, theories of change, situation and stakeholder analysis, and resource mapping:

- *Communication Strategy*, including media and other forms of outreach: It defines how the campaign will capture the attention of the target audiences and prompt them to take the action the campaign calls for. Strategic communication is results-oriented, evidence-based, "client"-centred, participatory, benefit-oriented (the audience perceives a benefit in taking the action proposed), multi-channel, high quality, and cost-effective (O'Sullivan et al., 2003. *A Field Guide to Designing a Health Communication Strategy*). Effective communication strategies are multi-pronged, targeting different audiences and audience segments through various mediums and channels, at different venues, and using different techniques.

- *Management and Coordination Processes* in campaign organisations and alliances must be defined at the outset.

- *Fundraising Strategy*: Establishing a realistic budget for the campaign and planning how best to raise necessary funding is a key element of success. Under-resourced campaigns may terminate prematurely without reaching their goal, demoralizing campaigners and their audiences.

- *Learning Strategy*: Monitoring campaign activities, the responses, and outcomes they provoke, as well as relevant external developments and changes in the campaign context are vital for effective campaign implementation. Furthermore, campaigns should generate learning for future campaigns through quality evaluation, documentation, and dissemination of findings.

- *Exit, Adaptation, and Scaling-Up Strategies:* What criteria must be met to end a campaign? What needs to happen at the end of a campaign? An exit strategy answers these questions. Scaling-up strategies determine when and how a campaign, e.g., a "pilot" campaign that introduces an innovative approach, can be expanded to a larger scale.

Successful campaigners educate themselves as much as possible about the following topics before taking action:

- The existing situation.

- Who is affected, positively and negatively, by the campaign issue?

- What changes could improve the situation?

- What resources, tactics, and tools are available to implement a campaign that will address the issue?

Campaigners use this information to develop their strategy, which guides them as they plan, implement, market, monitor, improve, and evaluate their campaign. The following questions should be addressed in a campaign's strategy:

Problem, Vision, Change

1. What problem are you confronting?
2. What is your vision of how the world will be once the problem is resolved?
3. What change(s) would bring about this vision?

Stakeholders, Relationships, and Targets

1. Who is affected, positively or negatively, by the problem?
2. How are these people or groups related to the problem and each other?
3. Who are you trying to reach?
4. If your campaign is successful, who will be affected?

It will be easier to develop your campaign strategy if you repeatedly answer key questions at each stage of your campaign. These questions should be about the problem and the solution, the stakeholders and targets, as well as the tactics, messages, and tools you will use. This section of this book can guide your actions, and your answers to these questions should be revised regularly as the campaign is implemented and the situation changes.

Create a Common Vision

If possible, include your entire campaigning group in identifying the problem and developing a vision for the changes you want to see. A shared understanding of the problem will stimulate ideas of possible actions to take and help your campaigning group remain motivated and focused throughout the process. Developing a shared vision will also assist in determining the best methods for monitoring and adjusting the campaign's implementation as necessary.

Activity 1: Problem - Solution - Change

1. Discuss and decide, as a group, what core problem your campaign seeks to address. Elaborate on all the adverse effects of this problem.

2. Each person in the group should answer the following question: What would a world without this problem be like?
o   Use words, diagrams, and illustrations.
o   Imagine unlimited resources (money, power, etc.).
o   Discuss and enumerate all the benefits of this proposed world.

3. Combine your individual visions of the future to create a single shared vision for the campaign. Discuss in depth which broad actions or changes would resolve the problem you identified to arrive at the world you have envisioned. These necessary actions are the main focus of your campaign. Discuss the scope of your campaign: decide whether it has multiple components (sub-campaigns). If it does, you may choose to narrow the focus of your campaign or create a multiple-campaign strategy.

Understand the Campaign's Stakeholders

Stakeholders are individuals, groups, organisations, or institutions involved in or affected by a particular issue. Your campaign may have their support, or they may be adversely affected by the issue in question. They may be able to influence the situation, or they may even be directly responsible for the problem you have identified. Obtaining as much information as possible about your campaign's stakeholders is critical in the campaign design process. You should do the following:

- Understand each stakeholder's relationship to the problem and your proposed solution

- Define the relationships between different stakeholders

- Determine the ability and willingness of stakeholders to help or hurt your campaign

- Identify which of these stakeholders your campaign should concentrate on to create the change you desire

Activity 2: Mapping Stakeholders and their Relationships

Begin by drawing a map on which entities with an interest in your issue are represented as circles or nodes, and lines connecting these circles represent the relationships between these entities and your issue. Sticky notes (post-it notes) are recommended for this activity because they can be moved around as needed.

1. Discuss the interaction at the heart of the problem that your campaign is attempting to solve. Who is the source of the problem? Who is affected by it? What is the nature of the connection between these entities, and why are they connected?

2. Continue in this manner, making notes as you go, until you have identified the interaction between entities (nodes) that best represents what you are attempting to change.

3. This step involves identifying all of the nodes for which this type of interaction is taking place.

4. These nodes should be placed in the centre of your map.

5. Identify the relationships between these central nodes and the other nodes on your map using the arrows. Start locally and work your way outward regionally, nationally, internationally, and even globally, if necessary, to achieve your goals. Depending on your problem, you may want to expand your map to include two or more levels of nodes (with each level clearly marked):

o   First Level: entities with direct contact to the central nodes (family/local)

o   Second Level: entities with contact to the first level (regional/national)

o   Third Level: nodes with general influence on the issue (international/institutional)

6. Draw lines between these nodes to represent relationships between them, and label each line with the type of relationship that exists; for example:

o   Power

o   Mutual benefit

o   Conflict

o   Potential

After you've identified as many stakeholders as you possibly can, you'll have a graphic representation of the relationships between your stakeholders and your issue. Following that, you should consider how your stakeholders might be able to assist you in achieving the change(s) you desire.

Activity 3: From Stakeholders to Targets

Begin by defining the specific goal(s) of your campaign or campaigns. Keep in mind the level of support and influence that each stakeholder has in relation to your campaign's objective or objectives.

1. Define what would be required to resolve your problem and bring about the change you seek in simple and actionable terms. You should set specific, measurable, and achievable goals while also being realistic and time-bound.

2. Using the list of stakeholders from the previous activity, identify as many individuals as possible who can assist you in achieving your goal.

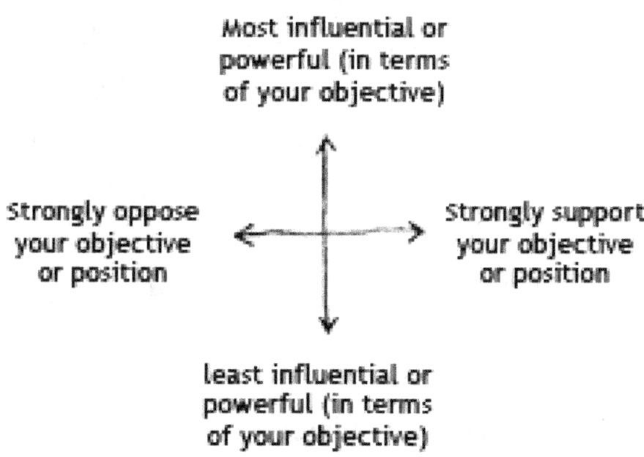

3. Create a horizontal and a vertical axis on a large sheet of blank paper by tracing them with a ruler (shown above). The stakeholders are grouped as follows:

o   The vertical axis represents their level of influence in achieving the goal of your objective, from most influential (top) to least influential (bottom).
o   The horizontal axis represents whether they are likely to oppose (left) or support (right) your campaign.

4. Then, after you've listed all of the stakeholders on a piece of paper, choose the most influential entities or individuals to serve as potential primary targets—or those who have the power to affect the change you're seeking. Make a note of their level of support or opposition to the proposed change in policy.

5. Discuss the relationships between these entities and the other parties involved. Depending on your stakeholder map from Activity 2, you might already have this information.

6. Make a list of the stakeholders who support your campaign and who have influence over or relationships with your primary target audience. You can think of them as secondary targets or participant groups who have the potential to become more actively involved in assisting your campaign in reaching its objectives. Figure out where they are on your graph and which two or three participant groups you want to focus on.

Activity 4: From Targets to Tactics

With the target audiences for your campaign identified and the relationships they have with other entities who are interested in the issue, you can begin to consider which tactics will best address your target and participant audiences.

1. Draw a half-circle divided into wedges. Place those who most support your campaign on the left side of the spectrum; those who oppose you the most on the right.

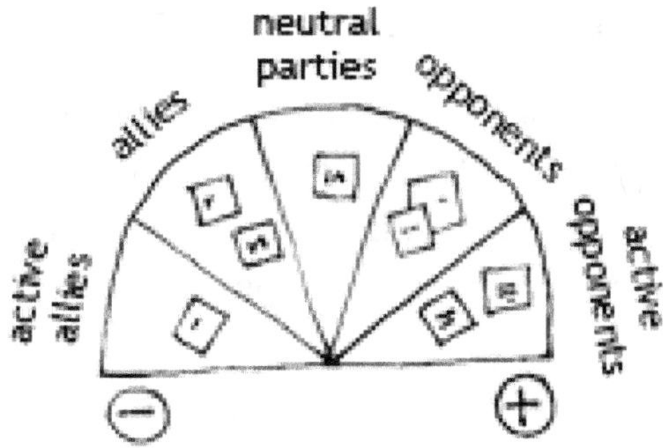

2. Place each target and stakeholder in a wedge according to their level of support for your cause, using your maps and sticky papers to aid you in this process. As a result, you have a spectrum of stakeholders, some of whom you have designated as primary or secondary targets. In a five-wedge diagram, you would have the following elements:

1. Active Allies: supportive and motivated to achieve your goals
2. Allies: may benefit from your success
3. Neutral Parties: may not be involved or affected currently
4. Opponents: may suffer from your success
5. Active Opponents: actively interfere with your activities
3. Use this diagram to help decide which tactics to consider, depending on each stakeholder's location on the spectrum. For example:
1. Supportive: use mobilisation tactics
2. Neutral: use educational, visualisation tactics
3. Opposing: use disruption, interference tactics

Campaign Strategies and Actionable Tips

According to experts, political campaign strategy should consist of **20% strategy** and **80% implementation**. As you embark on your political campaign journey, now is an excellent time to complete a significant portion of your strategy.

The earlier you start, the better. The most effective politicians are constantly managing and organising their campaigns (even if it is only in their own heads) by building relationships, determining their future campaign stance based on what they hear, and so on and so forth. However, suppose we are talking about your upcoming election. In that case, you will want to begin assembling your team and formulating your campaign strategy as soon as it is legally possible before the election date. All of your campaign elements, such as donations, the number of campaign team members, the number of voters contacted, and so on, will benefit from having more time to prepare.

Competitor Analysis

The evaluation of competitors is critical in any competition. A thorough understanding of your opponents' strengths and weaknesses can provide you with a significant advantage in developing your campaign messaging, participating in head-to-head debates, and undermining their campaign message when it becomes necessary.

Action Tip: Create a competitor analysis worksheet to help you track where you stand in relation to the other candidates running for the position. Make a spreadsheet with the strengths and weaknesses of all of the candidates, including yourself. On the same spreadsheet, list each candidate's positions on the key issues that will be discussed during the election. This enables you to identify your strengths and weaknesses and where you are vulnerable in relation to your competitors, and you can communicate more clearly with your customers.

Recognizing the Current Political Landscape

Before putting pen to paper on any strategy, it is important to look closely at the political landscape in which the election will be fought. We are living in a time of reactionary politics, in which liberal ideas will not be well received. Is the area's demographic makeup shifting, bringing in a more urban or progressive cohort that might be more receptive to progressive ideas than conservative ones? Is there a particular hot-button issue, such as immigration, that is dominating political debate at the moment? Are you an incumbent politician who has been tarnished as a result of something that occurred during your tenure in the position? If so, it may necessitate you taking the offensive against your competitors, or you may find yourself fighting a defensive campaign to remain afloat.

If you can grasp the general consensus among voters, as well as how media narratives influence or undermine that consensus, you will have a much stronger foundation upon which to build your strategy.

Digital Tools

There are various political campaign tools available to you that will be beneficial to your campaign. They are typically based on improving the shape and organisation of your team or are intended to improve your team's ability to communicate more effectively. I've compiled a fairly comprehensive list of the most popular tools used in place of traditional political party management software. I've used some of them personally and will share this list at the end of this section.

Field Organising

For most campaigns, field organising is a must. Whether this is done door-to-door or through 'hot-spot canvassing' in the community, it is an effective form of voter persuasion and GOTV strategy. Field organising strategy needs to be built by someone who has experience with voter targeting, canvassing techniques, and the tools that facilitate this. At a minimum, you will want to get a return on the investment of time and money into fieldwork translated into votes.

Obtaining Voter Data

Acquiring voter data should be straightforward but often is not. There are several places where you can begin your search. Your local authority should be able to provide you with a digital version of the electoral register. If not, ask them why not? You might be able to get a file from party sources (if you are a political party member) that has been worked on over time. Otherwise, you might be able to purchase a voter file from a third-party vendor (if this is legal in your jurisdiction). Failing all of these, a property register can suffice for getting started in building a voter database.

Voter Targeting

Quick question, do you know how many voters there are in your district? Do you know how many are likely to vote, or which of them are likely to vote for your competitor? Having answers to these questions will help as you begin your voter targeting work from the voter databases you have assembled. No campaign expects to communicate with everyone in their district. Ideally, you will speak primarily to those who are likely to vote and who are either your supporters or could be convinced to vote for you. If that group of people isn't big enough to get you elected, you should consider pulling out of the race!

Action Tip: Check your voter file for any indications of propensity to vote, previous voting history, or support level for your candidacy. If you don't have this, you are likely to waste a lot of time in your campaign learning about your electorate rather than persuading them.

Capturing Voter Issues

Everyone running for office has a 'sense' of what the electorate thinks. They usually try to respond to that understanding of voter issues with campaign messaging to represent those views. All of this is great, but in a digital era, it is possible to be a bit more rigorous about this and to capture voter issues in a way that accurately reflects those concerns and helps the campaign team. There are many ways this can be done, including online surveys, face-to-face canvassing, market research, and social media interaction. The critical component is to have a codified way of capturing raw data, perhaps into tags or hashtags. Tagging conversations with #education or #guncontrol will give your team a way to understand the entirety of your voter outreach in a simplified manner.

Funding Models

Assuming you don't want to re-mortgage your house to gamble on an election run, you will need some strategy for getting the money in to pay for your campaign. The most critical bit of research you can do is to monitor and copy what similar campaigns do in your district. Doing so will help you avoid breaking any funding rules while using tried and tested methods of generating revenue. Fundraising events, party stipends, and donation buttons on your website are common ways to raise money.

Action Tip: Set up your core campaign budget based on your lowest projections for donations/funding. Then, anything you raise above this figure can be channelled into scalable campaign spending like digital ads, billboards, paid canvassers, etc.

Who to Hire?

A big question for any candidate or campaign is, "Who should we hire?" This will be dictated to some extent by your budget but should also be based on getting the right person for the type of campaign you are running. You might be involved in a local campaign that needs someone with local knowledge and good contacts. Or you might be running a more extensive campaign that requires a higher level skill-set based around media appearances and voter polling. Key positions typically include campaign manager, campaign consultant, digital director, field director, and finance director. In their own way, all are valuable, but only you will know what you can afford and which positions might give you the best return.

Action Tip: Use our hiring matrix to figure out how to rank your necessary hires. Then match your budget with how many of those seats you can fill. Remember, you may be able to fill some of those roles from your own (voluntary) team.

Working on GOTV Strategy

Critical to your campaign strategy as a whole will be your election day and 'get out the vote' strategy. Think about how you will mobilize your supporters on polling day and what information you will need to have collected to do so. Capturing voting intention from voters can be done during canvassing and used on election day. Understanding your stronghold areas can help you do targeted work in those areas in the run-up to election day. Equally, any target demographics (like veterans or union members) can be targeted with advertising, email blasts, or face-to-face contact.

Online Properties

Your online properties—website and social media pages—will need to work hard for you to maximize your campaign. Setting them up can be time-consuming and expensive, so be very clear about what you need from the beginning. Some basic functionality includes a bio section, campaign messaging, a donation button, volunteer signup, and links to your social media properties. There are numerous website providers expressly set up for political campaigns, a list of which you can get in the resource below. There are also companies like NationBuilder and Crowdskout that provide website builders as part of their packages. Your social media profiles—Facebook page, Twitter accounts, Instagram, etc.—should fill in your campaign updates, responses to what is happening on the campaign trail, and provide brand awareness. It will be important to resource your digital campaign with people that have experience influencing voters online.

Voter Outreach

Voter outreach consists of canvassing, phone banking, attending town halls and public appearances, and email or digital communications. So, it's pretty broad! When composing a voter outreach strategy, the idea is to balance the amount of outreach you can do with the resources you have. You may have to be pragmatic about how many voter contacts can be achieved, but you should have a plan for how you will attack each of these areas. In some cases, one type of outreach may be more effective than others (tip: canvassing is the most effective method of getting votes). In other instances, voter outreach might be dictated by the resources at your disposal.

Action Tip: Request a plan of action from your outreach managers, i.e., your campaign manager, field director, and digital director. Each plan should be based on the number of weeks to election day.

Public Appearances

Public appearances are a staple of political campaigning. Whether through media interviews, political debates, or just a presence at community meetings, you will be required to regularly communicate with groups of people. There are some simple tips that you should get clear in your strategy from day one. Firstly, how much exposure can you get through public appearances? And secondly, do you know what to do when you get them?

The way to best prepare for media appearances is to speak in everyday language, have about three points that you want to deliver, and treat your interviewer/audience as your peer. In this way, you should be able to communicate effectively with anyone.

Action Tip: Try to obtain some media training at the beginning of your campaign. Failing that, if you are an Ecanvasser customer, talk to us to get feedback on your technique.

Personal Branding

In the previous chapter, I have made mentioned political brands. Like it or not, the campaign is personal. As a candidate, you embody the campaign's values—and you need to represent that in your public persona. Don't be afraid to take strong positions, and don't be too political. Voters want to see personality and for that personality to be consistent across social media, public appearances, and campaign messaging. It is essential to discuss the personal branding of the candidate at the beginning of the campaign, so it is strategic rather than just responding to what happens on the campaign trail—aim to be proactive, not reactive.

Action Tip: Research your audience, and set out your personal brand in terms of backstory and current positions on the issues. Have a kick-off meeting with your campaign team where you explain to them the personal brand that you are all working toward.

Campaign Team Onboarding

Your campaign team size will significantly impact your ability to campaign successfully. It is an important strategic element to aim for the highest possible number of volunteers and paid members of your campaign (that you can afford or manage, that is). Team onboarding drives can occur online or when meeting supporters, but a system should be in place to take someone from declaring an interest in becoming a team member right through to having them onboarded very quickly. This process can be handled through email if the appropriate system and structures are in place.

Action Tip: Build a template email that can be sent to anyone who declares an interest (and whose email is captured). This email will include requisite information and an invite to either a weekly campaign onboarding meeting or a campaign team software like Ecanvasser.

Combating Fake News

Fake news, misinformation, lies, whatever you want to call it, has been around forever in political campaigns, and they will continue to exist for the foreseeable future. Being able to respond to it appropriately means you will need to have both a social media presence and a public presence. Otherwise, you will be unable to counteract the false information. A great example of this inability to react to news occurred with Lockheed Martin in 2016 when Donald Trump tweeted that their F-35 program was plagued with cost overruns. Because they did not have very well-developed social media channels, it took several days to react to the tweet publicly. In the meantime, $1.2 billion had been wiped off their share price! Similarly, politicians need to respond to accusations or fake news quickly and provide hard evidence where necessary to refute those claims.

If your campaign feels that somebody is spreading fake news about you, it is advisable to challenge that publicly and get out ahead of the story. If you have developed your social media presence, you may find you can lead the conversation rather than react to what is happening.

Action Tip: Assemble a list of possible areas of misinformation that the campaign might come up against and develop clear responses or crystal clear campaign messages for those areas. Make sure you have solid social media channels that have connections to both media outlets and social influencers.

Campaign Messaging

Campaign messaging needs to be developed on each issue area with background information, the candidate's track record in this area, and details on their plan for that area in the coming years.

Once these have been filled out, the overall campaign message that incorporates the candidate's brand can be developed. Remember to be distinctive. Your messaging can be the same as your opponent's—but it does need to be delivered differently.

The 20 Best Campaign Software Platforms

Political parties and activist campaigns worldwide are shifting in response to technological changes in the way citizens and voters interact with the world around them. In every capital and regional centre, political parties are asking themselves the same questions:

How do we build a community engagement strategy? How can we build our party membership? What should our digital strategy be? How do we win the election?

Check out the below political campaign software platforms and tools that have proved effective for parties and politicians:

- **Slack** - If you haven't used Slack before, it's an excellent way for teams to communicate. It has a laptop interface that allows teams to share messages, documents, and images, and maintains fantastic office communications. It also has a great mobile app that allows you to connect all your field workers into the loop. You can create channels in Slack for, say, Precinct #4 Field Team or Voter Issues, and in this way, keep on top of all aspects of your campaign communications cleanly. Oh, and it's entirely free until a certain threshold of messages has been met (but you're unlikely to hit that level in a typical campaign).

- **YouTube** - YouTube needs no introduction, but it makes our list because so much content online is being consumed in video format. Candidates need to be in front of the camera, explaining their message and responding to what comes up on the campaign trail. These videos can be shared through social media and email subsequently. YouTube is a free product unless you want to promote your videos.

- **CallHub** - CallHub is an excellent telemarketing and text messaging software that connects to your voter database. Charges are based on the number of calls made—ideal for GOTV and general voter outreach. Plus, follow them on social media, and you can see they are made up of some truly dedicated and passionate staff!

- **Hotjar** - This might not be known to you, but Hotjar can record visitor interactions right on your website. See how visitors navigate your site, what they respond to, and what they skip over. It is amazing software for figuring out how to get people to donate to your site, sign up for a newsletter, or become a supporter. It also gives valuable information on the types of content visitors like, so you can cycle that intelligence back into your campaign. Free or €29 per month plans are available.

- **HootSuitc** - HootSuitc is a social media scheduling tool. We love this. Connect your Facebook, Twitter, and other social media to Hootsuite, and you can schedule content to go out at various intervals over the coming days and weeks. It has helpful auto-suggested content for you based on your preferences. HootSuite simplifies your social media efforts, which means you can get it all done in thirty minutes in the morning rather than checking in all day. It also means you can work on social media very openly with the rest of your team. It has a free plan but isn't hugely expensive if you want to go beyond what is offered there.

- **Click & Pledge** - Online fundraising can always be easier right? Finding a simple, straightforward way to improve online fundraising efforts is a common problem for our users, which is why Click & Pledge makes perfect sense. Customize and brand your fundraising campaigns with mobile-friendly donation forms, real-time receipts, and more. Embed them directly into your website or use a standalone link.

- **Hubspot Sales** - Don't be put off by the title; Hubspot Sales offers excellent functionality for teams requiring a task board and email tracking. Build around 'funnels' of individuals who can be imported (just with their email if necessary) into the CRM system. The idea is to move that person down the funnel to a stated goal, such as making a donation or becoming a supporter. It can be beneficial for targeted efforts like fundraising rather than for working with your voter database as a whole. It can help your campaign team to focus on individuals. Task management and email tracking (did they open my email? How many times?) are included, and the system easily connects to other software. Many campaign teams are using this now, but there needs to be a good return as it costs about $50 per person to use monthly.

- **Facebook** - What is there to say, really? Facebook pages are essential for all campaigns. It is your face to the world for many campaigns and the place where voters can interact with you. Facebook ads platform is also perfect for targeted advertising. If there is one social media platform to be involved with, it is FB. Additionally, FB Live is a live-streaming service that can be used for digital town halls, open meetings, or to drive engagement with voters on specific issues. It isn't going anywhere any time soon, that's for sure!

- **L2** - Running a successful campaign requires data. While the most reputable way to get this is usually from a government body, you can also purchase this information. L2 is probably one of the most commonly known organisations that provide this kind of service. Whether you are using an electoral register, party data file, or a purchased list, it will be your most important tool for direct outreach to voters and helping you better understand voters.

- **VoterCircle** - VoterCircle is a powerful and easy-to-use friend-to-friend outreach platform that enables your campaign team and supporters to leverage their personal relationships to benefit your campaign or organization. It is an effective tool for building your grassroots the way it should be done and getting the best from your GOTV operations. They have a free version, but also it can jump to $150 per month for some extra functionality.

- **Anedot** - Anedot is an excellent platform for managing donations. Fundraising is optimized with easy-to-use forms that embed right on your website. Pricing is based on a percentage of what you raise, so there are no initial costs.

- **Change.org** - Change.org is a simple petition-building tool that allows anyone, including campaigns, to sample the appetite for a particular issue or to gather support and connect with new audiences. Very simple to use, Change.org is something every campaign should take advantage of.

- **Twitter** - Another one that needs no introduction. Build your social media capital on Twitter, including an audience of followers. The ability to campaign with "just 280 characters" can be compelling and allows you to react incredibly quickly to campaign events. It brings you closer to your electorate but needs to be carefully managed. All tweets should be proofed before being sent. Free tool in monetary terms, at least.

- **Instagram** - Instagram has moved from the periphery to become one of the dominant social media channels. Instagram stories and reels allow you to share short videos, which is a great way to connect with a younger audience if used correctly. We are huge fans of the platform here at Ecanvasser HQ because there is endless potential. It allows you to build confidence in front of the camera using their Story functionality and easily connect with issues and movements using tags similar to Twitter.

- **Whatsapp** - Whether you like it or not, your campaign is already using Whatsapp. Experience tells us that field campaign teams use Whatsapp as a secondary communication tool. In many parts of the world, it is more important to capture Whatsapp contact info from voters for GOTV purposes than through the main communication channel. It is essential to consider this platform from the beginning and to set up Whatsapp groups as necessary rather than have it develop organically in the background in a way you don't have any control over. Free and fully encrypted messaging and video messaging service.

- **Survey Monkey** - This is the best-known online and email survey tool. It is a great way to get voter feedback and build campaign intelligence without significant outlay. Surveys can be built quickly and delivered by social media, website, email, and even mobile. It shouldn't cost more than €39 monthly

- **Intercom** - Intercom is one of those chat boxes you see on the bottom right of a website. It provides a simple Q&A interface with website visitors (i.e., voters) and allows you to deliver information, images, and other resources based on actions taken on your website. Having used this personally, I can say it is the best online tool of the past few years.

- **Ecanvasser** - Ecanvasser is a great way to get your team out in the field, door-knocking, and capturing voter information. Voter mapping, surveys, issue tracking, and a suite of analytics help you understand what voters are thinking and better organize your team. You can also connect your email blast functionality directly to your voter database and voter outreach for better email targeting. Tiered pricing makes it very affordable for local campaigns up to national races. It starts at just €19 monthly, including unlimited users.

- Tectonica - Tectonica is our full-service website design and digital strategy studio that builds the online tools you need for a successful campaign. They create brands, plan winning digital strategies, and produce the communication and organizing tools required for success.

- Nationbuilder - The original political software—Nationbuilder. From a single dashboard, campaign managers can build profiles of supporters and activists who subscribe to their website or interact on Twitter, integrate that database with information from social media and electoral rolls, rally their base using emails, texts, and voice calls, and organise canvassing according to target voters' location.

Election Campaign

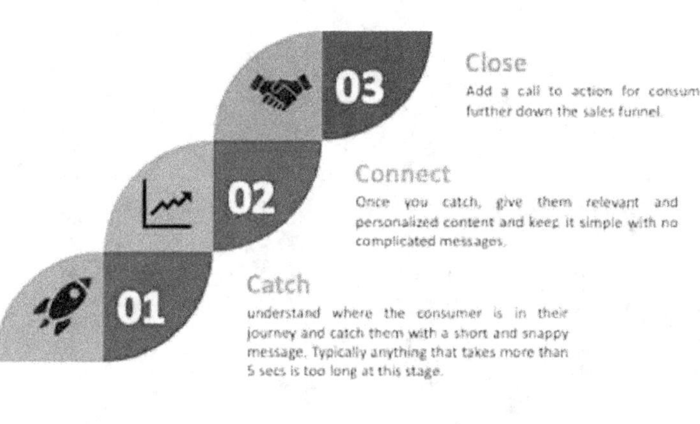

My-mindguide.com

Expected Political Participation

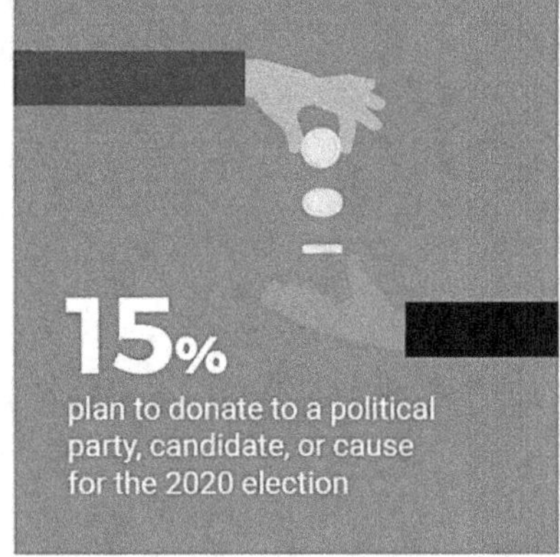

Chapter Five

Politics and Social Media

Throughout the previous chapters, I have touched on this subject in one way or another. Still, I will go into greater detail about politics and social media and how they tie into one another in this section. The use of social media in modern-day politics gives those who have it in their arsenal a significant advantage over those who do not. Anyone with an Internet connection can easily find praised for becoming a content creator, even more so for empowering their users to do so through social media. The concept of "new media populism" encompasses the ways in which users can include disenfranchised citizens and allow the general public to participate in political discourse in a more engaged and active manner. People's access to political information can be improved through utilizing new media, including social media platforms such as Facebook and Twitter.

Social media platforms and the Internet have made it easier to disseminate political information in opposition to mainstream media tactics, which are often centralised and top-down in nature and impose high entry barriers to those who wish to participate.

Social Media as a News Source

The use of social media platforms to access political news and information by adults and children alike has increased in recent years, particularly during election season. According to a Pew Research study conducted in November 2019, one-in-five adults in the United States get their political and election-related news primarily from social media platforms and 48 percent of adults in the United States rely on social media for this information, with the majority being between the ages of 18 and 29 years old.

Furthermore, Reddit, Twitter, and Facebook are the most popular social media platforms, with most users obtaining news information from them. Adults in the United States use the platform in 67 percent of cases, with 44 percent accessing the platform to get news.

According to the Reuters Institute Digital News Report published in 2013, the percentage of online news users who blog about news issues ranges between 1 and 5 percent. More people use social media to express their opinions on current events, with participation ranging from 8 percent in Germany to 38 percent in Brazil. However, online news consumers are more likely to discuss online news with their friends offline or to use social media to share stories without creating original content.

The rapid dissemination of information on social media, which is spread by word of mouth, has the potential to alter public perceptions of political figures in the short term with information that may or may not be accurate. Whenever political information is intentionally disseminated via social media, it can benefit campaigns. On the other hand, spreading false information about a political figure through word of mouth, or misuse by politicians, can be extremely harmful. For example, Congressman Anthony Weiner's use of the social media platform Twitter to send inappropriate messages contributed to his resignation.

Social Media as Attention Economy

The use of social media, particularly in connection with news disseminated through social media sites, contributes to the concept of the attention economy. The public will see, share, and otherwise digest and distribute news content that has garnered the most attention. "The resale of human attention," as Tim Wu of Columbia Law School puts it, is what he calls the attention economy.

Because of the abundance of ideas, thoughts, and opinions circulating through social media platforms, these communication platforms are persuasive in nature and frequently work to change or influence opinions when it comes to political views. As it has been discovered that news consumption leads to political influence, the greater the number of people who use social media platforms as news sources, the more their political opinions will be influenced. Despite this, people are expressing less trust in their government and others as a result of media consumption; as a result, social media has a direct impact on trust in media consumption. It has been demonstrated that reading newspapers increases social trust, whereas watching the news on television has been shown to decrease trust in other individuals and news sources. News media, particularly social media, play an essential role in democratic societies because they enable citizens to participate in political processes and debates. Consequently, when it comes to maintaining healthy democratic networks, the news must be accurate so that citizens' levels of trust are not adversely affected. For a democratic system to be healthy and well-functioning, it must have a certain amount of trust built into it.

With the increase in the amount of political news posted on various types of social media, younger generations are becoming more interested in politics. Because they rely more on social media than older generations, they are exposed to politics on a more frequent basis and in a way that is more integrated into their online social lives. While it is important to inform younger generations about current events in politics, there are many biases present in the world of social media. In May 2016, former Facebook Trending News curator Benjamin Fearnow admitted that his job was to "massage the algorithm." Still, he denied that any "intentional, outright bias" was perpetrated by either human or automated efforts within the organisation. Facebook fired Fearnow after it was discovered that he had leaked several internal company debates about Black Lives Matter and Republican presidential nominee Donald Trump.

Social Media as a Public Utility

Based on the premises of non-rivalry and non-excludability in consumption, there is a heated debate about whether or not social media is a public good. As a result of the rights of platforms such as Facebook and Twitter to remove content, disable accounts, and filter information based on algorithms and community standards, social media can be considered an impure public good because it can be excluded.

Arguments in favour of treating platforms such as Google as public utilities and public service providers include statements made by Benjamin Barber in The Nation magazine, such as:

To be effective equalisers, new media platforms must be treated as public utilities, with the understanding that spectrum abundance (the justification for privatisation) does not preclude monopoly ownership of hardware and software platforms, and thus cannot guarantee equal civic, educational, and cultural access to citizens.

On the other hand, Zeynep Tufekci argues that online services are natural monopolies that enable the "corporatization of social commons" and the "privatisation of our publics."

One argument that demonstrates the impure nature of social media as a public good is that control over content continues to reside in the hands of a small number of large media networks, such as Google and Facebook, among others. Both Google and Facebook can shape the environment in the name of personal and commercial goals that promote profitability rather than in the name of encouraging citizen participation and public debate.

Effect of Social Media on Democracy

Social media has been criticised as being harmful to democracy. This is not without a solid basis. Ronald Deibert states,

"The world of social media is more conducive to extreme, emotionally charged, and divisive content than it is to calm, principled considerations of competing or complex narratives."

On the other hand, Ethan Zuckerman believes that social media provides an opportunity to inform more people, amplify voices, and allow a diverse range of voices to be heard—and heard louder. When confronted with falsehoods, Mari K. Eder, retired general of the United States Army, points to the Fourth Estate's (the press and news media in explicit capacity of advocacy and implicit ability to frame political issues) failures, which have allowed outrage to be passed off as news, contributing to citizen apathy and further distrust in democratic institutions.

Politicians and Social Media

Social media has provided politicians with the ability to subvert traditional media outlets by directly engaging with the general public. Donald Trump took advantage of this when he lost the 2020 presidential election, claiming that the election was fraudulent, thereby necessitating the need for a re-election campaign. The consequences of Trump's online actions were demonstrated on January 6, when supporters of the former president launched an attack on the United States Capitol.

Being a popular presence on social media can also increase a politician's chances of being elected. For example, when Boris Johnson ran for Prime Minister in the U.K. 2019 election, he had more than half a million page 'likes' (significantly more than the other candidates). This alone meant that when he released his launch video, it received more than 130,000 views, which could have been a significant factor in him eventually being elected.

In a study conducted by Sounman Hong in connection with politicians utilising social media and whether the consequences would be largely positive or negative, it was determined that in the case of backbenchers, 'underdogs,' and opposition, an increase in use was found to help them gain recognition and support from the public eye where they would otherwise go unnoticed.

Democratisation

The Arab Spring

During the height of the Egyptian Revolution in 2011, the Internet and social media platforms played a critical role in disseminating information about the situation as it unfolded. Hosni Mubarak was the president of Egypt at the time, and he would go on to lead the country for nearly thirty years. As a result of the enormous power that the Internet and social media gave the people, Mubarak's government shut down the Internet using the Ramses Exchange in February 2011.

Egyptians used social media sites such as Facebook, Twitter, and YouTube to communicate and organise demonstrations and rallies in support of the overthrow of President Hosni Mubarak. According to statistics, the rate of Tweets from Egypt increased from 2,300 to 230,000 per day during this period, and the top 23 protest videos received approximately 5.5 million views.

Disinformation in Connection with a U.S. Election

Although fake news can benefit consumers, such as confirming far-right beliefs and spreading propaganda in support of an electoral candidate, it also has significant negative consequences on a personal and societal level. Examples of social costs to consumers include the spread of disinformation, which makes it more difficult for consumers to seek out the truth. As was the case during the 2016 election, it makes it more difficult for consumers to choose an electoral candidate. The findings of a 2017 Congressional Research Service study were summarised as follows: "Cyber tools were also used [by Russia] to create psychological effects in the American population. Correspondingly, there is a high likelihood that these activities will compromise the integrity of information, sow discord and doubt in the American public about the validity of intelligence community reports, and raise questions about the democratic process itself."

The marginal social cost of fake news is exponential; as soon as the first article is shared, it will have a small impact on a small number of people, but as the article is spread more widely throughout Facebook, the negative externality grows quickly and powerfully. The quantity of news demanded can therefore shift up during election season as consumers seek accurate information; however, it can also shift down as people have less trust in the mainstream media. A Gallup poll conducted in 2016 found that "Americans' trust in the mass media 'to report the news fully, accurately, and fairly' was at its lowest point in the organisation's polling history, with 32 percent expressing confidence in the media's ability to do so." Furthermore, Republican and far-right political viewers have a lower level of trust in the mainstream media, with only 14 percent expressing confidence in it. According to a survey conducted by the Pew Research Centre between June 16 and 22, approximately 72 percent of American adults believe that social media companies have excessive control and influence over politics today. Among those polled, only 21 percent believe that the power held by these social media companies over today's politics is the appropriate amount, with 6 percent believing that it is insufficient.

Algorithms have the potential to speed up the spread of misinformation through social media platforms. Algorithms take into account users' previous behaviour and engagement activity to deliver them content tailored to their specific interests and beliefs. In these online spaces, algorithms are frequently used to create echo chambers and to sow radicalism and extremist thinking.

A high level of 'engagement' on social media is encouraged by algorithms, which means posts that receive many "likes" or "comments/replies" are encouraged. Engagement and controversy are inextricably linked, for better or worse. However, "Benford's Law" of controversy states that "passion is inversely proportional to the amount of real information available." Controversy garners attention because it elicits an emotional response. Therefore, the less grounded in facts a political tweet is, the more engagement it is likely to receive, and the greater the likelihood of spreading misinformation.

Twitter has risen to prominence as a forum for political debate. According to psychologist Jordan Peterson, Twitter has a radicalising effect, as revealed during a GQ interview conducted with him. He explained that for any given tweet that appears on one's 'feed,' the tweet will have been seen by a far greater number of people than is reflected in the number of likes and comments on the tweet. Who, then, are the individuals who leave comments on a tweet? It is expected that those who comment will be those who exhibit the strongest opinions on the subject and who want their voice to be heard. This, according to Peterson, creates an environment in which the opinions expressed by the average user do not accurately reflect the views of a representative sample of the general public. The opinions that are most frequently expressed on Twitter are those of people who are at either extreme end of the political ideology spectrum, which is known as the 'radicalising effect.'

U.S. Election Interference

The 2016 United States Presidential Election served as an example of how a state actor, in this case, Russia, used social media to influence public opinion. In order to leak fake news stories with headlines such as "FBI agent killed after leaking Clinton's emails" and "Pope Francis endorses Donald Trump," various tactics such as propaganda, trolling, and bots were employed. In one study, researchers discovered that pro-Trump fake news was four times more prevalent than pro-Clinton fake news and that bots generated a third of pro-Trump tweets. Furthermore, social media has made it possible to collect vast quantities of information about social media users, which can then be used to make inferences and predictions about what information and advertising the user is most likely to be exposed to in the future. This was brought to light in 2018 as a result of the Cambridge Analytica Facebook investigation. The company's data and predictions were used to sway voters during the 2016 Brexit/Leave campaign and the 2016 U.S. presidential election Trump campaign, among others.

This scandal first made headlines in 2016 as a result of the Brexit referendum results in the United Kingdom and the presidential election results in the United States, but it was a long-running operation by Cambridge Analytica with the permission of Facebook. According to Alexander Nix, who previously served as Cambridge Analytica's Chief Executive Officer of Market-Research Operations, these techniques became known to the public, causing the scandal. A video in which he admitted to working directly with Donald Trump to gather information on the American electorate was released on March 20, 2018, prompting his suspension from his company, which he had established in 2013.

According to a 2016 presentation by Nix, shifting the focus away from demographics and geography for targeted advertisements and instead focusing on psychographics to target personality traits and gain a better understanding of voter demands has proven to be more effective in gaining votes for Ted Cruz in 2016. In 2016, one of Nix's business associates, Steve Bannon, left the company to take over Donald Trump's presidential campaign. As a result of the video leak that cost Nix his job, it is widely assumed that Bannon had a direct influence on the campaign. In addition to this, Cambridge Analytica employees were heavily involved in the Vote-Leave campaign for the 2016 Brexit referendum, according to the company. Many people believe that the involvement of a targeted advertising organisation in two populist campaigns that produced shocking results represents a potential threat to democracy, and they are right to be concerned.

However, this is not the only instance of possible election interference via the use of social media. Rodrigo Duterte was elected President of the Philippines on November 1, 2015, after being hailed as "the first person to fully harness the power of social media." Since the previous election, Facebook's popularity had skyrocketed. Duterte saw this as an opportunity to recruit social media influencers to promote his party and create viral content, demonstrating social media's influence on democracy.

Back to Cambridge Analytica: On May 18, 2017, Time magazine reported that the United States Congress was looking into Cambridge Analytica in connection with Russian interference in the 2016 presidential election in the United States. According to the report, CA's microtargeting capabilities may have been used to coordinate the spread of Russian propaganda throughout the world. When Facebook was revealed to have improperly used the personal information of over 50 million Facebook users while working on Trump's presidential campaign, The Times of Israel reported that the company had used what Nix called "intelligence gathering" from British and Israeli companies as part of their efforts to sway the election results in Trump's favour. However, social media is now a medium that makes this type of interference possible. This was the work of a single company, and regulations may be able to prevent this in the future.

Election Results

As of October 2020, candidates will be prohibited from claiming victory until their election victory has been credibly projected by news outlets or officially certified by the government, according to Twitter's new policy.

Impact on Elections

The use of social media has a significant impact on elections. Social media is frequently used in conjunction with traditional mass media networks, such as cable television. Many people rely on cable television as their primary source of information and sources, as well as their first point of contact with those sources. Partisanship and predispositions to certain political parties are fuelled by commentary on cable television, which is also fuelled by partisanship. Social media takes messages from the mainstream media, amplifies and reinforces them, perpetuating partisan divides in the process, among other things. According to a study published in the Journal of Communication, social media does not have a significant impact on people's opinions or votes, but it also does not have a minimal impact on people's opinions or votes. Instead, social media produces a bandwagon effect, which occurs when a candidate in an election makes a mistake or achieves great success. When this happens, users on social media will greatly magnify the impact of that failure or success.

According to the Pew Research Centre, nearly one-fourth of Americans learn something about presidential candidates from an Internet source such as Facebook or Twitter. Nearly one-fifth of the population of the United States uses social media, with two-thirds of those Americans between the ages of 18 and 29. Rallies and movements are frequently sparked by the youth's presence on social media platforms. For example, during the 2008 presidential election, a Facebook group with 62,000 members was formed to support the election of President Obama. Within days, rallies of thousands of students were held at universities across the country. Rallies and movements of this nature are commonly referred to as the "Facebook Effect." On the other hand, social media can often have the opposite effect and have a negative impact on many users.

According to a poll conducted by the Pew Research Centre, nearly 55 percent of social media users in the United States say they are "worn out" by the number of political posts they see on social media. That number increased by nearly 16 percent following the 2016 presidential election, largely due to the continued rise of technology and social media. Nearly 70% of people say that discussing politics on social media with people on the other side of the political spectrum is often "stressful and frustrating," compared to 56% who expressed this sentiment in 2016. The number of people who describe these discussions as "interesting and informative" has decreased from 35% to 26%.

When it comes to the influence of social media on the youth vote, the evidence is quite compelling. In the 2018 elections, nearly 31% of the youth cast ballots, compared to only 21% in the 2014 elections. The use of social media among teenagers continues to grow, with approximately 90 percent of teenagers using at least one social media platform. Of that 90 percent, 47 percent received information about the 2018 elections through a social media platform like Facebook or Twitter. In contrast to receiving a message directly from the candidate's campaign, the messages shared on social media platforms frequently included messages encouraging people to register to vote and actually cast their ballot. Therefore, of the first-time youth voters who cast ballots in the 2018 election, 68 percent obtained their information about voting from social media platforms. This is in contrast to the traditional methods of being notified to vote, which were used by only 23 percent of first-time voters in the past.

Furthermore, only 22 percent of youth who did not learn about an election through social media or traditional means were very likely to vote; on the other hand, 54 percent of youth who learned about an election through social media or traditional means were very likely to cast a ballot. Many political groups and foreign governments have created fake accounts to disseminate a large amount of misinformation to divide the country, as reported by Forbes. As a result, young people are becoming increasingly sceptical of what they read on social media. The information seen on social media is frequently filtered. According to the Pew Research Centre, the number of people who get their news from social media has increased by 62 percent since 2008. On these social media sites, a large number of algorithms are in operation, filtering the information that individual users are exposed to. The algorithms learn about a user's likes and dislikes, and then they begin to tailor their feed to reflect those preferences. As a result, an echo chamber is created. For instance, black social media users were more likely to see race-related news. Additionally, in 2016 the Trump campaign used Facebook and other platforms to target Hillary Clinton's supporters to drive them out of the election and take advantage of such algorithms.

There is disagreement over whether or not these algorithms impact people's voting decisions and their political views. Iowa State University finds that for older individuals, even though their access to social media is far lower than the youth, their political views were far more likely to change from 1996 to

2012, which indicates that there is a myriad of other factors that impact political views. Further, based on other literature, the research indicates that Google has a liberal bias in its search results. It is estimated that these biased search results can affect an individual's voting preferences by nearly 20 percent. In addition, 23 percent of an individual's Facebook friends are of an opposing political view. Nearly 29 percent of the news they receive on the platform opposes their political ideology, indicating that these new platforms' algorithms do not create total echo chambers.

According to Washington State University political science professor Travis Ridout, in the United Kingdom, the popular social media platforms of Twitter, Facebook, Instagram, and YouTube are beginning to play a significant role in campaigns and elections. Contrary to the United States, which allows television ads, in the United Kingdom, television ads are banned. Thus, campaigns are now launching massive efforts on social media platforms. Ridout furthers that the social media ads have more frequently become offensive attack ads aimed at other politicians. Social media can provide many individuals with a sense of anonymity that enables them to get away with such aggressive acts. For example, ethnic minority women politicians are often the targets of such attacks.

In the United States, many youth conservative voices are often reduced. For instance, PragerU, a conservative organisation, often has its videos taken down. On a different level, social media can also hamper many political candidates. Media and social media outlets frequently publish stories about breaking news that is both controversial and popular to increase traffic.

One prominent example is President Donald Trump, whose controversial statements in 2016 often drew the attention of many people, thereby increasing his popularity while simultaneously shunning the other presidential candidates.

During the 2020 Presidential Election, both campaigns heavily utilized social media. In terms of Twitter users, President Donald Trump had nearly 87 million followers at the time, while Vice President Joe Biden had 11 million. However, the top tweets from Biden have outperformed those from Donald Trump by nearly two to one, despite the significant difference in popularity between the two. There were 6.6 million mentions of Trump and Biden on Twitter between October 21 and October 23, with Biden claiming a 72 percent share of the mentions during that period. As a result, Biden received nearly twice the number of mentions as Donald Trump during the 2020 Presidential Debates, with nearly half of those mentions being negative. For Trump, some of his mentions were also negative, which was unfortunate for him.

In Europe, social media has less impact than it does in the United States, which is a good thing. According to the European Parliament, only 34% of the Members of the European Parliament (MEPs) use Twitter, compared to 68% who use Facebook. Compared to the other political parties, the European People's Party (EPP) had the most extensive social media following in 2012, with 7,418 followers. This is in relation to the 375 million voters who make up the entire European Union. When comparing the impact of social media following in the United States, former President Obama has more than 27 million fans. At the same time, the highest in Europe is former

French President Nicolas Sarkozy, who has more than 700,000 fans, a significant disparity. The 2008 U.S. presidential election heightened the importance of using technology in politics and campaigns, particularly social media, and the need for more people to do so. Since then, Europe has followed their lead and has seen an increase in the use of social media platforms.

When it comes to analysing the role of fake news on social media, there were approximately three times as many fake news articles that were pro-Trump as pro-Clinton articles. While there were 115 pro-Trump fake news articles and only 41 pro-Clinton fake news articles, pro-Trump stories were shared 30.3 million times on Facebook, while pro-Clinton stories were shared 7.6 million times. It is estimated that each share generates around 20 page visits, which means that with approximately 38 million shares of fake news articles, there are 760 million page views for those articles. This means that each adult in the United States visited a fake news website three times.

Even though European politicians do not use social media platforms to the same extent that Americans do, this does not rule out the possibility that social media platforms will play a significant role in European Politics—particularly in elections— in the future. Extremists used social media platforms in the run-up to the 2017 German Bundestag Elections to gain support for the far-right Alternative für Deutschland (Germany's Alternative for Germany). Despite their small numbers, the group was able to publish "patriotic videos" that made it onto the YouTube Trending tab and trending the hashtag "#AfD" on social media sites such as Twitter. Even though Alternative für Deutschland was predicted to come in fifth in the election, they ended up with 13.3 percent of the vote, placing them as the third largest party in the Bundestag and becoming the first far-right party to be elected to the chamber since 1961.

Whether the spread of fake news impacts elections remains contentious because more research is needed, and it is difficult to quantify the consequences of fake news in elections. However, several things have been shown when it comes to assessing real versus fake news. For starters, individuals over the age of 65 who are more conservative are more susceptible to being influenced by fake news. These individuals are also more likely than other individuals to believe false information. Also, identifying whether or not an article shared on social media is fake news is difficult for college students to do. Additionally, a person's political party affiliation and ideological beliefs can be used to predict their conspiratorial beliefs. For example, those who voted Republican or held a more conservative belief are far more likely to believe in baseless theories like the idea that former President Obama was born outside of the United States. Those who voted Democratic or held more liberal beliefs are more likely to believe in conspiracy theories like former President Bush playing a role in the September 11th attacks.

Advertisements

Many political advertisements, such as those urging people to vote for or against a specific candidate or to take a position on a particular issue, are now being distributed through social media platforms. On November 22, 2019 Twitter announced that it would no longer facilitate political advertising anywhere in the world going forward. In order to take advantage of the fact that social media provides different information to different people depending on their interests, advertising methods such as "microtargeting" and "black ads" have become popular. These methods allow advertising to be much more effective for the same price when compared to traditional advertisements such as those on cable television.

Grassroots Campaigns

Political referendums are frequently the subject of social media campaigns at the grassroots level, with individuals rallying around issues such as abortion rights. These campaigns are especially effective when it comes to feminist political issues, as studies have shown that women are more likely than men to tweet about policy issues and do so in a more aggressive manner than their male counterparts. Like-minded individuals can come together to influence social change and use social media as a tool for social justice by banding together and collaborating. For instance, the referendum to challenge Ireland's Eighth Amendment in connection with abortion law is an example of this.

Organizations from civil society, such as TogetherForYes, have used Twitter to bring abortion law into the public eye and make the dangers of the Eighth Amendment visible and understandable. This is because individuals and advocates came together at the grassroots level to make their voices heard. As social media spreads beyond the local level to have a widespread global political impact, the issue of strict abortion laws has become a global issue rather than one that is only relevant to Ireland and the United Kingdom only. The increased mobilisation of participants in a political grassroots campaign on social media is the campaign's greatest strength. Given that social media platforms are largely accessible, it is possible to provide a political platform to voices that have been traditionally silenced in the political sphere or traditional media.

Concise Scenarios of How Social Media Enhances Political Campaigns

Political parties across the globe are learning that along with advertising on traditional mediums such as television and newspapers, they must invest in digital marketing if they want to compete with their rival parties. Over the past few years, we've seen an uptake in U.K. and U.S. parties, in particular, using social media campaigns to defeat their opponents. Here, I will highlight how three high-profile political marketing campaigns leveraged digital marketing to successfully promote their nominee.

1. Donald Trump: Making Digital Great Again

You may recall that I mentioned Trump and Cambridge Analytica previously. In this chapter, I'll go into additional detail specifically regarding Trump's digital campaign, which is perhaps the most visible example of political digital marketing in recent history. Though it was certainly divisive, no one can deny that the former President of the United States' campaign was extremely effective. Many people believe it helped him win the election.

Brad Parscale is a key figure in Trump's digital marketing campaign. He is the CEO of Trump's digital efforts and the founder of the Giles-Parscale agency. The entire Trump digital team was based in San Antonio and consisted of 100 people with jobs ranging from copywriters to web developers and data scientists, among others.

As a member of Trump's inner circle, Parscale was one of the few people permitted to tweet from the President-Elect's personal Twitter account, @realDonaldTrump.

Prior to Trump, he had little experience promoting political candidates, but this apparent lack of experience allowed him to approach it as if it were a typical B2C digital campaign. "I always wonder why politicians act as if this stuff is so mystical," Parscale had indicated. "It's the same sh*t we use in commercials, just with fancier names." The digital operations division was the Trump campaign's largest funding source, with massive amounts of Facebook and email donations flooding in.

The campaign kicked off with a $2 million investment in Facebook advertisements. He began by uploading the names of Trump supporters he discovered on Facebook. Then he targeted others who shared similar characteristics, such as activity or demographics. These "Like Audiences" were critical to the campaign's success. However, other types of content, such as tens of thousands of different targeted web pages, also played a role. In total, Trump's digital team generated or created over 100,000 unique pieces of content.

However, Trump did not have enough projected votes to win. It wasn't until the final weeks of the election that this changed dramatically, resulting in his victory. We now know how he did it, thanks to some senior members of the President's team. Essentially, he accomplished his goal by targeting young women and African Americans with $150 million in Instagram and Facebook advertisements in the weeks leading up to the election.

Trump's team launched Project Alamo, a custom database containing detailed identity information for 220 million Americans and 4,000 to 5,000 individual data points about each person's online and offline life. (As far as we know, this database still exists today.) Trump's team used this wealth of data to launch a massive digital ad campaign to discourage Hillary Clinton's supporters from voting across the Facebook Audience Network, Facebook, Instagram, and Facebook data-broker partners. "We have three major voter suppression operations in the works," a senior Trump official told BusinessWeek reporters. "They're aimed at three groups Clinton needs to win overwhelmingly: idealistic white liberals, young women, and African Americans."

Some of these ads are said to have been distributed through Facebook "dark posts," which are non-public paid posts shown only to specific users to exploit religious and racial differences. This is where things get complicated. Many of these ads, such as the one below, were allegedly created by Russians to undermine the election and benefit Trump.

When asked if "fake news" ads helped Trump win the election, Facebook founder Mark Zuckerberg initially denied the allegations but later changed his tune, saying, "After the election, I made a comment that I thought the idea that misinformation on Facebook changed the outcome of the election was a crazy idea," Zuckerberg said, referring to a previous denial that Facebook could have influenced voters. "That was a dismissive remark, and I regret it. This is far too important an issue to dismiss."

The Trump campaign spent roughly $70 million per month on advertisements, far more than Democratic opponent Hillary Clinton. And in this case, we believe digital marketing made a significant difference in the razor-thin final vote. Democratic turnout on Election Day was surprisingly low, particularly among sporadic and first-time voters in key battleground states.

2. U.K. Labour Party Learns from Its Past Mistakes

The 2017 General Election in the United Kingdom was a close race, but the Labour Party came out on top, gaining 21 seats from its Conservative opponents. Though Jeremy Corbyn did not win the Prime Minister's seat, the Labour Party made significant progress by investing in effective digital media campaigns aimed at delivering the right messages at the correct times.

According to a late-2016 Demos poll, 23% of U.K. adult social media users believed that social media platforms helped them "understand parties' policy positions" before an election, and 26% believed social media engagement makes them more likely to vote. That was something Labour noticed in 2017. According to the Electoral Commission, the Conservative Party spent £1.2 million on Facebook advertising ahead of the 2015 General Election, while Labour spent seven times less. For the next two years, it regretted its decision.

The year 2017 was a departure for the party. It began to invest heavily in social media, realising that it is an important part of winning a political race. The party even developed its own social media targeting tool, Promote, to tailor specific policy messages to individual voters. The system generated over a thousand unique variations of core policy messages, which were delivered based on a variety of factors, including location. In addition, Labour leader Jeremy Corbyn became the first politician of his generation to use Snapchat to document his political journey. He was also a frequent user of Twitter and other social media platforms. Though Corbyn did not win the Prime Ministerial election, he successfully persuaded the public to give the Labour Party significantly more seats and a 40% share of the vote. He was also extremely popular among the younger generation.

The Labour Party concentrated on spreading positive messages about party leaders and policies, a sharp contrast to its negative criticisms of the "Tories" during the 2015 general election.

In the weeks leading up to the election, its website featured a temporary homepage with the number of days until the election highlighted and the urgency messaging clearly outlined. These tactics are frequently used successfully in digital marketing campaigns for retail/eCommerce sites, and they were effective here as well.

Labour spent a lot of time and effort, in addition to its website, expanding its reach on social media. "In the six weeks following the announcement of the 2017 General Election, 'We Are Social' revealed that the Labour Party increased its following by 61 percent across social media platforms such as Twitter, Facebook, and Instagram," according to Croud.com. In the same period, the Conservatives' social media following increased by only 6%." The party used positive messaging, celebrity endorsements, and advertisements to encourage young voters to vote. In the final 24 hours of the registration period, a record 622,000 people registered to vote, many of them being young people.

Momentum, a grassroots Labour party organisation, spent only £2,000 on Facebook advertising, compared to the Conservatives' £1m, but had significantly more success because the ads were highly targeted and positive in nature, whereas the Conservatives remained quite negative and failed to engage their audience.

3. Leo Varadkar Takes a Firm Stance on Tough Issues

In June 2017, Leo Varadkar, an Irish Fine Gael politician, was elected Taoiseach, Minister for Defence, and Leader of Fine Gael. Digital marketing, particularly in online videos, played a significant role in his success. Mr. Varadkar believes that social media will play a "key role in the modernization of Government communications" and has used it extensively since taking office. Varadkar's website is simple to navigate and contains all of the information needed to make an informed decision about a political candidate, such as an About section outlining his political stances, links for voter registration, and a Newsletter sign-up to keep people informed.

He was also very active on social media during the campaign, particularly on Facebook and Twitter, where he used the hashtag #CampaignforLeo. The hashtag was frequently accompanied by videos featuring high-profile individuals explaining why they supported Varadkar. According to Philip Ryan of The Irish Independent:

"In fact, the entire Varadkar campaign has been a masterclass in political campaigning. Everything from the early groundwork with the parliamentary party to their campaign video has been miles ahead of Coveney's team in terms of organisation and presentation."

Following his election, the Taoiseach is known to post weekly videos on Facebook outlining his progress in office. He intersperses these political updates with glimpses into his personal life on Twitter.

****

Generally speaking, politicians from all political parties worldwide recognise the importance of social media in communicating directly with voters and in having a significant impact on the outcomes of their campaigns. A wide variety of targeting options and customised messages for hundreds of different audiences are available through paid social media advertisements. It is where the real power lies for any modern-day politician committed to winning the election.

For the time being, I commend you for having the courage to read this far. In closing, I'd like to point out that, as new technological breakthroughs are made on a regular basis, the subject of political marketing is becoming increasingly effective.

However, contrary to popular belief, new technologies are not as determinative as techno-determinist approaches would have it. As opposed to this, they impact society to the extent that the characteristics of the cultural, political, economic, and historical conditions in which they thrive are taken into consideration.

Many people will be perplexed as to why my book contains so many examples and references from the United States and the United Kingdom, and I understand their confusion. Perhaps it is because I am European, and most of us are only concerned with these references? No, that is not the case. I enjoy politics and literature from all over the world, and I am interested in current events. Because these countries are the most advanced when it comes to political campaigning, I chose them as examples because they are the most adept countries when it comes to political marketing. We can all learn from them, both in the positive and negative aspects of campaigning (i.e., what to avoid).

****

If you enjoyed this title and would like to read about other topics that have changed my life, please check out my new books on Amazon or my website:
www.my-mindguide.com.

Also, let's stay connected on social media. Please drop a line on Facebook or Instagram, and stay tuned for updates! You're welcome to share your thoughts with me directly as well: gassner@my-mindguide.com. In return, I'll send you a gorgeous infographic that you can cut out and frame.

Also, please leave a review on Amazon, as this will help me to reach an even broader audience. Thank you so much for your time, insight, and undying hunger for knowledge!

Acknowledgements:

Thank you to all of my colleagues, clients, friends, and family members, who have contributed their own energy, time, and encouragement to make me what I am now.

I also want to say thank you to Gabriel Palacios, the King of Hypnotherapy and a Swiss bestseller author who taught this old fox new tricks, letting me deep-dive into the mystery of hypnotherapy. I learned so much along the journey that I'm now a certified master-hypnosis coach and conversation coach myself!

Furthermore, I thank the fantastic teachers of SAMYANA/Bali who trained me to become a certified yoga and meditation teacher.

Last but not least, I give a special thanks to my master-teacher Eckhard Wunderle, who's close to a saint to me. He introduced me to the world of meditation and let me discover all the wonders it has to offer. I couldn't be more proud about having received my certification as a meditation teacher from directly from him at the Institut für Spirituelle Psychologie.

Thank you for the time being.

Author's Bio

Kurt Friedrich Gassner has worn many hats throughout his lifetime, including but not limited to serial entrepreneur, Creative Director, Meditation Teacher, Licensed Hypnotherapist, and more recently, self-improvement author. Leveraging his treasure trove of experiences and in-depth knowledge of psychology, he provides his readers with the tools they need to unlock their infinite potential.

As a prolific self-help writer, Kurt has authored the following books: *The Power of Forgiveness, Lie or Die, Soul-Match, Can You Inherit a Poisoned Mind?* and *The Power of Poverty*. He also authored a best-selling children's book in German-speaking countries and has over 20 books underway.

When it comes to enduring success, Kurt understands that financial prosperity isn't the only aspect one should strive for. He may be a self-made millionaire, but what really transformed his life is mastering his unconscious mind. Perseverance, personal power, self-awareness, and learning from past mistakes have all been key ingredients to bringing his dreams to fruition—and he strives to impart that wisdom onto others through his writing.

During his spare time, Kurt Friedrich Gassner is either travelling across the globe, golfing, biking in the Alps, hiking, or spending quality time with his loved ones. For the last 37 years, he has been happily married and he is the father of two successful children. Presently, he resides in both Munich, Germany and Kirchberg, Austria.

REFERENCES

1. https://en.wikipedia.org/wiki/Human_nature#:~:text=Human%20nature%20is%20a%20concept,'means'%20to%20be%20human.

2. https://www.elitedaily.com/money/the-power-of-fear

3. Edinburgh Review, March 1829, p. 185.

4. https://www.apa.org/news/apa/2020/fear-motivator-elections

5. 'Instinct is usually defined as the faculty of acting in such a way as to produce certain ends without foresight of the ends and without previous education in the performance.'—W. James, Principles of Psychology, vol. ii. p. 383.

6. Reflections suggested by the New Theory of Matter, 1904, p. 21. 'So far as natural science can tell us, every quality of sense or intellect which does not help us to fight, to eat, and to bring up children, is but a by-product of the qualities which do.'

7. Ethics, Bk. viii. chap. I. φ•σεɩɩ τ᾽ •νυπ•ρχειν •οικε ... ο• μ•νον •ν •νθρ•ποις •λλ• κα• •ν •ρνισι κα• τοɩ•ς πλε•στοις τω•ν ζ•ων, κα• τοɩ•ς •μοεθν•σι πρ•ς •λληλα, κα• μ•λιστα τοɩ•ς •νθρ•ποις ... •οικε δ• κα• τ•ς π•λεις συν•χειν • φιλ•α, κα• ο• νομοθ•ται μα•λλον περ• α•τ•ν σπουδ•ζειν • τ•ν δικαιοσ•νην.

8. Diary of Madame D'Arblay, ed. 1905, vol. iv. p. 184, 'If they even attempted force, they had not a doubt but his smallest resistance would call up the whole country to his fancied rescue.'

9. https://en.wikipedia.org/wiki/Culture_of_fear

10. PUTIN'S PATH TO POWER (forthcoming in POST-SOVIET AFFAIRS) By Peter Rutland

11. https://www.loc.gov/classroom-materials/elections/presidential-election-process/persuading-voters-political-campaigns/

12. Craig, G. 2004. The Media, Politics and Public Life> Maryborough, Victoria, Australia: Ullen & Unwin.

13. Henneberg, S.C. 2004. Political Marketing Theory: Hendiadyon or Oxymoron. Working Paper Series.

14. Mareek, P. 1995. Political Marketing and Communication. London: John Libbey & Co.

15. Marshment, J.L. 2006. Political Marketing as Party Management-Tatcher in 1979 an Blair in 1997. Keele University

16. https://online.pointpark.edu/public-relations-and-advertising/political-marketing-strategies/#

17. McNair, B. 2003. An Introduction to Political Communication (Second Edition, Ed). New York: Routledge

18. Newman, B.I. 1999. The Mass Marketing of Politics: Democracy in an Age of Manufactured Images. California: SAGE Publications, Inc.

19. Ugur, Gokhan. 2012. Americanisation of Political Communication Practices. Canadian Social Science. Vol. 8 No. 3

20. Stephen Henneberg, Political Marketing Theory: Hendiadyoin or Oxymoron, University of Bath, 2004.

21. Stephen Henneberg, Geenric Functions of Political Marketing Management, University of Bath, 2003.

22. Phil Harris, Matthew Ward, Marketing the mayor: political marketing and the election campaign, Government and Public Affairs,2005.

23. Jennifer Lees-Marshment, Political Marketing as Party Management - Thatcher in 1979 and Blair in 1997,Keele University

24. Phil Harris,Andrew Lock,and Terese Nievelt, Perceptions of Political Marketing in Sweden: A Comparative Perspective, Ottago university,2005.

25. https://en.wikipedia.org/wiki/Spin_(propaganda)#:~:text=Public%20relations%20advisors%2C%20pollsters%20and,might%20have%20on%20public%20opinion.

26. https://archive.informationactivism.org/basic1.html

27. https://www.ecanvasser.com/campaignblueprint/
political-campaign-strategy/

28. https://theconversation.com/the-vomit-principle-the-dead-
bat-the-freeze-how-political-spin-doctors-tactics-aim-to-shape-
the-news-106453

OTHER BOOKS BY THE AUTHOR

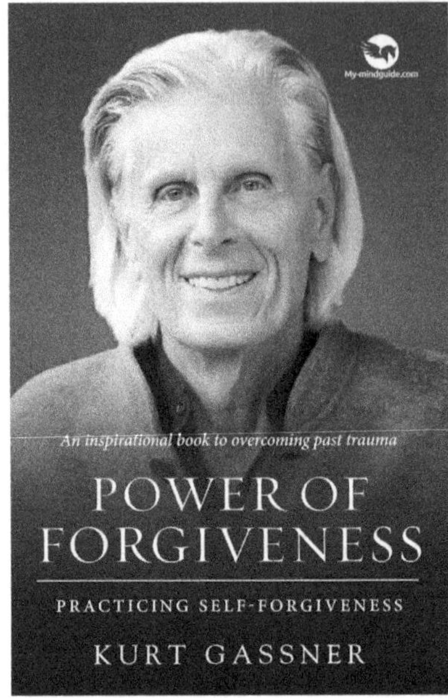

OTHER BOOKS BY THE AUTHOR

OTHER BOOKS BY THE AUTHOR

OTHER BOOKS BY THE AUTHOR

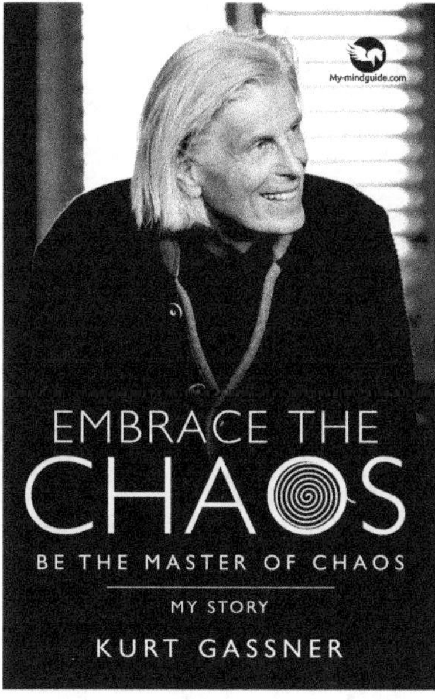

My-mindguide.com
ECKO
FIRED FOR SUCCESS?
TRUE STORIES AND MANAGEMENT LESSONS
FOR OUR TOUGH CHANGING TIMES
KURT GASSNER

My-mindguide.com
ECKO
WEGEN ERFOLG GEFEUERT
Eine wahre Geschichte über das Scheitern in Unternehmen und
was junge Führungskräfte aus einer Fehlerkultur lernen können.
KURT GASSNER

My-mindguide.com
Unlocking
The Healing
Power of Pets
What Pets Can Tell You About Your Soul
KURT GASSNER

My-mindguide.com
Heilkraft
Unserer
Lieblinge
Was Haustiere über Ihre Seele verraten können
KURT GASSNER

My-mindguide.com
THE
BLISS OF
STRUGGLE
WINNING STRATEGIES
FOR DEMANDING TIMES
KURT GASSNER

My-mindguide.com
STARK
DURCH
„STRUGGLES"
DAS IDEALE MINDSET,
UM KRISEN ZU MEISTERN
KURT GASSNER

My-mindguide.com
LIE LYING
& LIAR
A LIE HAS NO LEGS BUT IT HAS WINGS
KURT GASSNER

My-mindguide.com
LÜGE LÜGEN
& LÜGNER
EINE LÜGE HAT KEINE BEINE, ABER SIE HAT FLÜGEL
KURT GASSNER

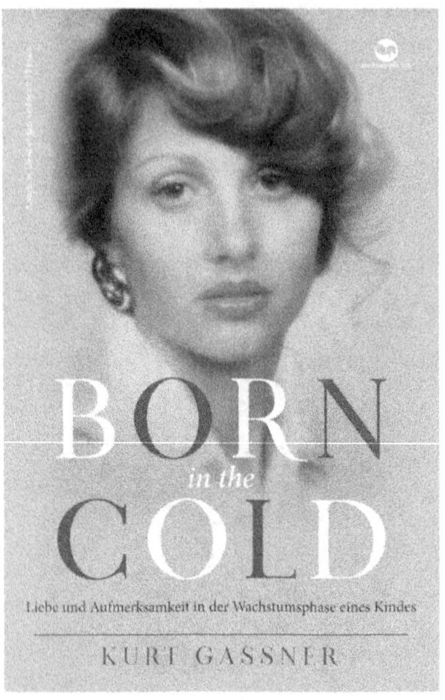

BORN
in the
COLD
Liebe und Aufmerksamkeit in der Wachstumsphase eines Kindes
KURT GASSNER

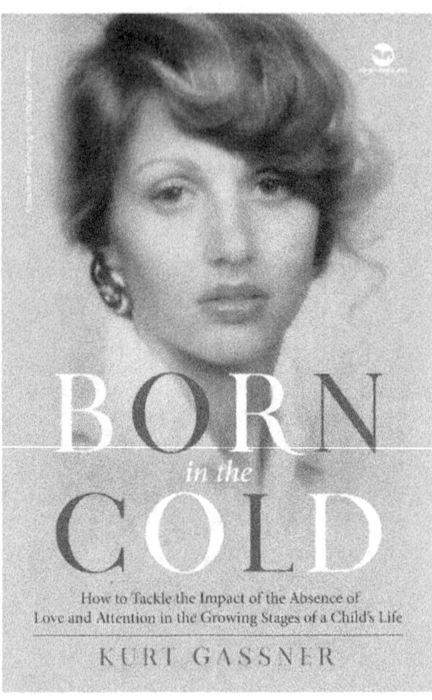

BORN
in the
COLD
How to Tackle the Impact of the Absence of
Love and Attention in the Growing Stages of a Child's Life
KURT GASSNER

SOPHIAS WUNDERWELT
10 ERZÄHLUNGEN
KURT GASSNER

SOPHIA'S WONDERWORLD
10 TALES
KURT GASSNER

BESTSELLING AUTHOR OF
The Art Of
FORGIVNESS
AMAZON #1 BESTSELLER
My-mindguide.com
A practical guide for self healing and overcome past traumas
The Art Of
FORGIVNESS
KURT GASSNER

Discover The Power Of Media In Politics And Its Effect On Voting Behaviour!

The media have played an important role in politics since the First Amendment established freedom of the press. Voters need information to make educated decisions, and the media's job is to give it to them.

Citizens learn about politics primarily from television and newspapers. These media outlets can influence voters by choosing which stories to cover.

In their daily routine, all citizens partake in mass communication. This communication takes place in various channels, such as radio, television, websites, social media, etc. Extensive research has shown that these contacts with media content may have effects on the cognitive, affective, behavioral, and even physiological levels. Such media effects are of special significance where they are intended by political stakeholders aiming to alter public opinion or influence and mobilize voters.

Introducing "How to win your Vote" By Kurt Gassner - A True Story About Political Marketing!

Sometimes we don't even realize that we are being brainwashed or influenced by the media. Our opinions are controlled and influenced by those who control the media. If you discover who controls the media, you discover who controls your mind.

In this book, Kurt Gassner is sharing a true story about helping his tax advisor become the mayor of Kitzbühel 19 years ago, and maintaining his position up until today! With his story, he aims to show you how politicians are made and that if you play the political marketing game right you can achieve your goals!

Top 3 Key Takeaways From This Eye-Opening Book:
✓ Discover Who Are The People That Run The Big Campaigns
✓ Explore What Tricks They Use To Convince People To Vote For Them
✓ Find Out How Politicians Are Made

Click "Add To Cart Now" & Explore The Secret Side Of Political Marketing!

I m an Austrian Enterpreneur and worked 40 years in advertising, brand consulting. I founded ad agencies in Munich, Vienna , L.A. (with Dhalan Netch Creative) and Zurich. Today I still run a

Network Publishing company www.trendguide.info and an Investment Company Trendguide Capital.

I used the Corona lockdowns and crisis to study Hypnotherapie and I m now a licenced Hypnotherapist (NGH,US, Switzerland, Germany) a Yoga and Meditationteacher

My-mindguide.com